Cornerstone Curriculum

Official Certification Edition
Mentor's Guide

Cornerstone Curriculum Official Certification Edition Mentor's Guide

© 2023. The Urban Ministry Institute. All Rights Reserved.

The Urban Ministry Institute
3701 East 13th Street North
Suite 100
Wichita, KS 67208

ISBN: 978-1-62932-063-2

Published by TUMI Press
A division of World Impact, Inc.

The Urban Ministry Institute is a ministry of World Impact, Inc.

CORNERSTONE

The
Urban
Ministry
Institute
a ministry of
World
Impact,
Inc.

Cornerstone Curriculum
Official Certification Edition

Alvin Sanders | Rev. Dr. Don L. Davis
Rev. Terry G. Cornett | Rev. Ryan Carter

*So then you are no longer strangers and
aliens, but you are fellow citizens with the
saints and members of the household
of God, built on the foundation of the
apostles and prophets, Christ Jesus himself
being the* **cornerstone**, *in whom the
whole structure, being joined together,
grows into a holy temple in the Lord. In him
you also are being built together into a
dwelling place for God by the Spirit.*

~ Ephesians 2.19-22

TUMI Press
3701 East 13th Street North
Suite 100
Wichita, Kansas 67208

Table of Contents

Part III: Ministry & Mission

Unit One: Christian Ministry

Unit Two: Urban Mission

Introduction to the Cornerstone Curriculum, Official Certification Edition

Welcome to the *Cornerstone Curriculum*, your new opportunity to be equipped for effective ministry in the Church!

The Challenge: Great Need, No Time, Few Funds

The harsh reality faced by anyone equipping pastors and lay ministers serving in at-risk communities is that of scarcity. Money and time are too scarce and too short for these valiant leaders to engage in a long, structured study who serve God in poor communities. They do extraordinary work often while holding down a full-time job and growing ministry. Many thousands of urban Christian workers who would benefit from our premier, comprehensive, seminary-level curricula like the *Capstone Curriculum* don't have either the availability or the funds to complete it. (The average time for bi-vocational students to finish *Capstone's* sixteen modules is three to four years.)

Meeting the Challenge: The *Cornerstone Curriculum*

To meet this great need, we have designed this unique curriculum, the *Cornerstone Curriculum*. Selected from specific, targeted lessons taken from *Capstone*, and adding Dr. Alvin Sanders's *Redemptive Poverty Work*, we created this course of study for those who will never have the time or funds to complete our more extensive *Capstone* set. The time to complete *Cornerstone's* three parts is the equivalent of only three *Capstone* modules. We created this resource to help these students access helpful resources without sacrificing quality or their ministry opportunities. *Cornerstone* will dramatically cut both the time and expense associated with typical Bible school or seminary studies or even the *Capstone Curriculum*, with no loss to either our fidelity to biblical truth or practical ministry training.

Be Equipped to Plant, Pastor, and Serve the Church!

Cornerstone's lesson materials combine the *Redemptive Poverty Work* course with material distilled directly from *Capstone's* modules, drawing out its essential truths from its four department areas (Biblical Studies, Theology and Ethics, Christian Ministry, and Urban Mission). We put together *Cornerstone's* lessons to provide you with a timely, cost-effective, and solid training regimen. Our training will provide you with certification, enrich your knowledge of the Scripture, and outfit you to minister effectively as a pastor, lay leader, or a Christian worker where you live and work. God has called and gifted you, and we hope to see you fulfill his calling on your life, that you may honor our Savior in everything you do.

I challenge you, therefore, to fulfill the Lord's ministry for you, all in the spirit of Paul's admonition to Timothy, "Do your best to present yourself to God as one approved, a worker who has no need to be ashamed, rightly handling the word of truth" (2 Tim. 2.15, ESV). Know that if you do present yourself to God as one approved, you will fulfill his call and bear spiritual fruit that honors Christ and pleases God. May God richly bless you in your studies, your discipleship, and your ministry!

With bold confidence in God's eternal Word to heal and transform,

Dr. Don Davis
Wichita, Kansas
February 1, 2023

Part I

Redemptive Poverty Work

Mentoring Part I:
Redemptive Poverty Work

Your first session will be an orientation. This is part of the class requirements for the students, and attendance is mandatory. In this session you will provide the expectations of the class, the grading policy, when assignments are due, and how quizzes will be administered, etc. If this is an online course using World Impact U (WIU), you will also orient the students to WIU, how to answer forum questions, and how to submit assignments.

There are also two videos to show the class during this session:

- *An Opportunity to Learn Redemptive Poverty,* Dr. Don Davis

- *The Dirty Little Secret of Poverty Work,* Dr. Alvin Sanders

Here are some suggestions as to what to cover in this first session:

Welcome

1. Open in prayer.

2. Provide your full name and Email address so that the students know how to reach you.

3. Remind the students that they should already have copies of the books:

   - *Redemptive Poverty Work,* Dr. Alvin Sanders

   - *Uncommon Church: Community Transformation for the Common Good,* Dr. Alvin Sanders

4. Allow students to introduce themselves, their ministry, and what they hope to get out of the class.

Introduction

Video: Watch the video *An Opportunity to Learn Redemptive Poverty,* by Dr. Don Davis, on how we need a clear, biblical, and compelling perspective on what it means to conduct life-affirming care in communities of poverty.

Introduce Redemptive Poverty Work Concept

1. *Redemptive Poverty Work* was developed from reviewing a "Redemptive Frame" and applying it to World Impact. A Redemptive Frame states

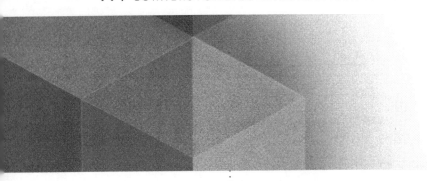

that there are three ways you work throughout the world: Exploitatively, Ethically, and Redemptively. You then take this frame and put it on top of your non-profit and the work that you do. Since World Impact does poverty work, working with people in communities of poverty, we have *Redemptive Poverty Work* (RPW).

2. Christianity was birthed out of people who lived in conditions of poverty, and to this day the overwhelming majority of people who ascribe to Christianity live in the condition of poverty. So it's very important to understand what Christ's view of the condition of poverty was and how he expected us to minister in it.

3. Now that we have RPW, World Impact has discovered that this is not only going to help the people with whom we already minister, but it is also opening doors to totally new audiences who would have never listened to us or even saw the reason to listen to us before.

4. Here are some examples:

   - There is a group of energy providers in the Atlanta, Georgia, area where we had connections with them previously. When Dr. Sanders presented RPW to this secular audience they loved it. So much so, that several CEOs of Public Utility Companies have reached out to see how they can partner with World Impact.

   - Dr. Sanders did a pilot training of RPW for two of the largest churches in Louisville, Kentucky, and they loved it because they discovered they had been doing a lot of toxic poverty work.

   - A missions pastor of a large church with several satellite churches said that RPW is how he could share the heart of service at his church.

5. This is for anybody and everybody who's interested in following the model of Jesus Christ and working with people who are in poverty, whether you're in poverty now or have never been in poverty. The only thing you need is an interest in working in communities of poverty as Christ worked in communities of poverty. It could be

a donor, an inner city pastor, a volunteer worker at a food pantry, a teacher, etc.

6. The mindset that we are developing for redemptive poverty work is to be able to look and act as Jesus did with us of creative restoration through sacrifice. For the people we are working with, we want to be able to provide pathways of opportunity, and to help them to understand that they can be used by God and to exist within the condition that they find themselves. Some may choose to try to better themselves and others may never get out of the situation they are in. What we can't forget is regardless of their material possessions, God loves them, and God is with them to use them.

7. The goal of this course is to have a practical theology of how to do successful redemptive poverty work.

Course Description and Syllabus

Review Course Description, Objectives, and Syllabus (found on pages 15-18 of the Student Workbook).

The following are some key points to make about each lesson:

- Lesson 1: *A Brief Theological Reflection*

  This lesson is not meant to be a thorough insight of everything the Bible has to say about people in poverty and the condition of poverty. Instead, if asked why are we doing this, you will have a practical theological answer.

- Lesson 2: *Toxic Poverty Work*

  In this lesson, we talk about the problem of toxic poverty work, which comes directly from an exploitative mindset.

  We will discuss how this can be an unconscious mindset, and that good intentions are not enough. Each person must engage their moral attitudes and mindset as to why they are doing poverty work and ask, "Is it biblical?"

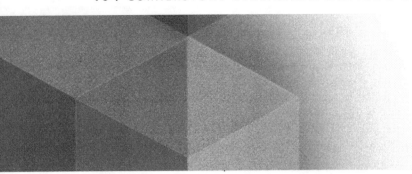

- Lesson 3: *Redemptive Poverty Work*

  In this lesson we define exactly what redemptive poverty work is, what it is about, and how it differs from toxic poverty work.

- Lesson 4: *Rhythms of Life and Poverty Work*

  Our final lesson shows how we can use eight spiritual disciplines to enhance our walk as a believer in Jesus Christ and prevent burnout.

Forum and Forms

Ensure students have access to the forum and to the forms they will need to complete their assignments. (These forms can be found online on the WIU Redemptive Poverty Work Dashboard.)

- Assignment Checklist

- Reading Completion Sheet

- Scripture Memory Grading Form

- Class Schedule with Assignments and Due Dates

Review the forms, forum use, and course requirements with the students.

Introduction to Redemptive Poverty Work

As a final step in this class session, watch *The Dirty Little Secret of Poverty Work.* which gives an overview of the three major approaches to serving individuals and families in at-risk communities, i.e., Exploitative, Ethical, and Redemptive, and lays the foundation for your entire training. Understanding the principles and practice of redemptive poverty work is essential for all those seeking justice and peace in communities of poverty.

Remind the students of their next class meeting and any assignments that need to be completed before the Lesson 1 class meeting.

Cornerstone Part I: *Redemptive Poverty Work* Course Schedule
Season, Year (ex. Fall 2021)
Name of Instructor
Date Range of the Class (ex. Nov. 17 - Dec. 22, 2021)

Meeting Information	Lesson and Assignments
Orientation Session	
Face-to-Face Meeting Date Time	***Orientation Session: Course Introduction*** Participate in Face-to-Face Meeting for Course Introduction
Session 1	**Lesson 1, A Brief Theological Reflection**

Face-to-Face Meeting
Date
Time
	Students should complete the following before this meeting:
	
	1. Complete Lesson 1 of *Redemptive Poverty Work* in the Student Workbook.
	
	2. Review questions at the end of the *Content* section of Lesson 1. Be prepared to discuss your answers in our Lesson 1 Face-to-Face Meeting.
	
	3. Complete the assignments in the *Assignments Due* section for Lesson 1 **before** our Lesson 1 Face-to-Face Meeting. Those assignments are as follows:
	
	  a. Read the following in *Redemptive Poverty Work*:
	    • *Introduction (pages 11-15)*
	    • *A Brief Theological Reflection (pages 17-22)*
	
	  b. Read the following in *Uncommon Church*:
	    • *Foreword* by Efrem Smith
	    • Chapter 3: *Jesus Did, Not Jesus Would: Jesus and the Condition of Poverty*
	    • Chapter 6: *Faith and Works: Eliminating the Tension between Evangelism and Justice*
	
	  c. Complete your summary of the readings on the *Reading Completion Sheet* for each reading listed above.
	
	  d. **Memorize Matthew 25.45** and grade yourself using the *Scripture Memory Grading Form*.
	
	After Face-to-Face Meeting:
	Take the Lesson 1 Quiz.

Meeting Information	Lesson and Assignments
Session 2	**Lesson 2, Toxic Poverty Work**

Face-to-Face Meeting
Date
Time
	Students should complete the following before this meeting:
	
	1. Complete Lesson 2 of _Redemptive Poverty Work_ in the Student Workbook.
	
	2. Review questions at the end of the _Content_ section of Lesson 2. Be prepared to discuss your answers in our Lesson 2 Face-to-Face Meeting.
	
	3. Complete the assignments in the _Assignments Due_ section for Lesson 2 **_before_** our Lesson 2 Face-to-Face Meeting. Those assignments are as follows:
	
	   a. Read the following in _Redemptive Poverty Work_:
	     • _Toxic Poverty Work (pages 23-30)_
	
	   b. Read the following in _Uncommon Church_:
	     • Chapter 2: _What Would Jesus Do? Poverty Is a Condition, Not an Identity_
	     • Chapter 7: _There Goes the Neighborhood: Understanding the Powers That Be_
	
	   c. Complete your summary of the readings on the _Reading Completion Sheet_ for each reading listed above.
	
	   d. **_Memorize Luke 4.18-19_** and grade yourself using the _Scripture Memory Grading Form_.
	
	After Face-to-Face Meeting:
	Take the Lesson 2 Quiz.

Meeting Information	Lesson and Assignments
Session 3	**Lesson 3, Redemptive Poverty Work**

Face-to-Face Meeting
 	
Date
 	
Time
	Students should complete the following before this meeting:
	
	1. Complete Lesson 3 of *Redemptive Poverty Work* in the Student Workbook.
	
	2. Review questions at the end of the *Content* section of Lesson 3. Be prepared to discuss your answers in our Lesson 3 Face-to-Face Meeting.
	
	3. Complete the assignments in the *Assignments Due* section for Lesson 3 **before** our Lesson 3 Face-to-Face Meeting. Those assignments are as follows:
	
	   a. Read the following in *Redemptive Poverty Work*:
	
	      • *Redemptive Poverty Work (pages 31-36)*
	
	   b. Read the following in *Uncommon Church*:
	
	      • Chapter 4: *The People of God: God's Plan for a Broken World*
	
	      • Chapter 8: *Championing the Community: Empowering Grassroots Leaders and Workers*
	
	      • Chapter 10: *The Kingdom Is in Us*
	
	   c. Complete your summary of the readings on the *Reading Completion Sheet* for each reading listed above.
	
	   d. ***Memorize John 1.14*** and grade yourself using the *Scripture Memory Grading Form*.
	
	After Face-to-Face Meeting:
	
	Take the Lesson 3 Quiz.

Meeting Information	Lesson and Assignments

Session 4
 	
Face-to-Face Meeting
Date
Time
	Lesson 4, Rhythms of Life and Poverty Work
	
	Students should complete the following before this meeting:
	
	1. Complete Lesson 4 of *Redemptive Poverty Work* in the Student Workbook.
	
	2. Review questions at the end of the *Content* section of Lesson 4. Be prepared to discuss your answers in our Lesson 4 Face-to-Face Meeting.
	
	3. Complete the assignments in the *Assignments Due* section for Lesson 4 **before** our Lesson 4 Face-to-Face Meeting. Those assignments are as follows:
	
	  a. Read the following in *Redemptive Poverty Work*:
	    • *Rhythms of Life and Poverty Work (pages 37-50)*
	
	  b. Read the following in *Uncommon Church*:
	    • Chapter 1: *Advocacy Is Not Enough*
	    • Chapter 5: *Doing Healthy Church: Seven Habits Toward Spiritual Maturity*
	    • Chapter 9: *Chasing Wild Dreams: Examples of Faith, Hope, and Love in Action*
	
	  c. Complete your summary of the readings on the *Reading Completion Sheet* for each reading listed above.
	
	  d. **Memorize Acts 2.42** and grade yourself using the *Scripture Memory Grading Form*.
	
	After Face-to-Face Meeting:
	
	  a. Take the Final Exam.
	  b. Complete the Course Evaluation Form.

Date	**Final Assignments Due** 1. Final Exam 2. Redemptive Poverty Work Course Evaluation Form

Note: Find an editable version of the above schedule on the World Impact U *Redemptive Poverty Work* dashboard. Edit the details for your class and distribute to your students.

Cornerstone Part I:
Redemptive Poverty Work
Course Survey

We greatly value your input and are here to serve you! Please answer the following Questions to give feedback on the training you received and who you are. The better we understand who you are and what you need, the better we can craft our resources and programs for your benefit.

While we prefer this form to be completed online, circumstances may prevent this from being possible. Please scan the completed forms and send to the Cornerstone representative.

1. Church, Ministry Network, or Organization

    What is the name of the organization that hosted this course?

2. How likely are you to recommend this course to a close peer or colleague? Please select 1-5

    5 = Definitely would recommend

    4 = Probably would recommend

    3 = Might recommend

    2 = Probably would not recommend

    1 = Would not recommend

Please answer questions 3, 4, and 5 based on the following rating scale:

    5 = Exceeded my expectations

    4 = Slightly above my expectations

    3 = Met my expectations

    2 = Slightly below my expectations

    1 = Did not meet my expectations

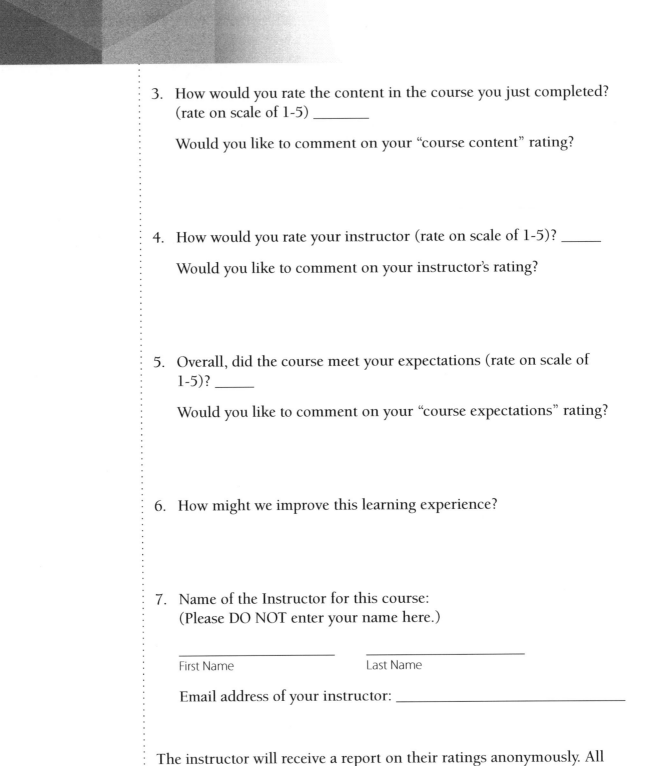

3. How would you rate the content in the course you just completed? (rate on scale of 1-5) _____

Would you like to comment on your "course content" rating?

4. How would you rate your instructor (rate on scale of 1-5)? _____

Would you like to comment on your instructor's rating?

5. Overall, did the course meet your expectations (rate on scale of 1-5)? _____

Would you like to comment on your "course expectations" rating?

6. How might we improve this learning experience?

7. Name of the Instructor for this course: (Please DO NOT enter your name here.)

_____   _____
First Name   Last Name

Email address of your instructor: _____

The instructor will receive a report on their ratings anonymously. All names and detailed information will not be shared with them.

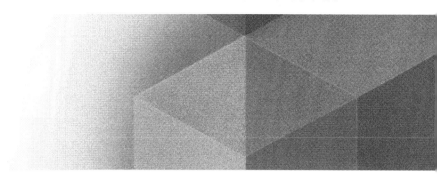

Personal Information

None of this data will be shared with your personal information attached. This is simply for data collection.

First Name:

Last Name:

Email Address:

Are you currently incarcerated (please circle one)? Yes / No

Sex/Gender (please circle one): Male / Female

Ethnicity (please select one of the following):

    a.   Asian/Pacific Islander

    b.   Bi-racial, Multi-racial

    c.   Black

    d.   Latino

    e.   Native American

    f.   White

Birth Year (e.g., 1976): _____

Thank you for completing this survey!

A Brief Theological Reflection

1
page 31
Lesson Introduction

Welcome to the Mentor's Guide for *Redemptive Poverty Work*, Lesson 1: *A Brief Theological Reflection*. This lesson provides a simple practical theology for poverty work. Specifically, this lesson emphasizes three biblical themes that undergird why we do what we do. As you lead your students through these biblical themes, make sure to give ample time to the Scriptures themselves. Students should understand clearly that Redemptive Poverty Work is rooted in Scripture. Help them to engage the Old Testament principles of empowerment and to truly consider Jesus's own favor for the poor and warnings against riches.

Christians are much more likely than non-Christians to view poverty as the result of personal failure. This mentality leads to the poverty-stricken being treated as "projects" instead of people to serve, which is not what God intended. It is the aim of this lesson to provide a biblical corrective to these attitudes and assumptions. The Bible gives significant instruction concerning how we are to treat those in poverty. Throughout this lesson, and the lessons to come, keep Scripture central for your students.

2
page 34
Summary

Emphasize the importance of biblical literacy.

1. There's been a complete flipping of people's ability to engage Scripture and apply it, and a heavy emphasis on advocacy and advocacy alone being the answer as to what ails people who live in the condition of poverty.

2. We should not try to divorce the two:

   • Believe in evangelism AND justice.

   • Believe in individual sin and systemic institutional sin.

3. We want to be champions and conveyors of that theological truth.

4. Biblical illiteracy is at an all-time high within our pews. Even for common biblical stories like Noah and the ark or Joseph and his brothers, half of those in church would not know about these. Don't assume that people know the Bible. If people don't generally know the Bible, then they definitely don't know what it says about poverty or the condition of poverty.

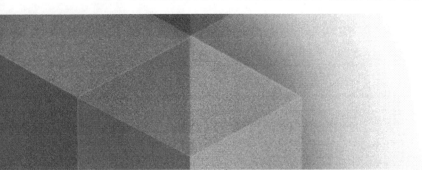

📖 3
page 34
Outline Point I

I. Poverty Is a Theme in Both the Old and New Testaments

The following are key insights to note as you discuss this section with your students.

1. The Bible is a book of the working poor.

2. Poverty is a lack of financial resources for people to be able to take care of the needs that they have in their life.

3. The Bible gives us many reasons for a lack of these resources.

    • Personal sin – example is the prodigal son. He had plenty of money but blew it all because of his attitude and character.

    • Societal/Institutional sin – people are in poverty simply because of the society that they live in; things that society does to keep certain groups of people in poverty and liberate others financially.

4. It's not either/or; it could be both/and.

5. In the USA, statistically most people in poverty were born into it and most of them don't switch poverty classes. (NOTE: This may be different in your country.)

6. The working poor is a theme that is woven throughout the Bible. The focus was not on how people got into that condition, but rather how can we create pathways of opportunity.

📖 4
page 34
Outline Point A

A. Old Testament Principles of Empowerment

Help your students understand the following:

1. The Old Testament focused on creating pathways of opportunity.

2. The Bible is not necessarily focused on causation. The Old Testament focused on creating pathways of opportunity for people to be able to survive their condition or transcend their condition

and understand that God is bigger than the circumstances they find themselves in.

- An example of this is a church that provided full tuition scholarships for God-loving kids in poverty, who had the potential and interest of going to college, but not the opportunity. With getting a college degree, they have become productive members of society and are no longer in poverty.

3. The Bible could have been situated in the condition of poverty to begin with because in almost every culture, you are looked down upon if you don't have enough resources (a second-class citizen).

- In the Bible, the nation of Israel wasn't looked at as a powerful nation, but a ragtag group of people who were in slavery. But God said they, the underdog, were going to be his people. The whole point of the book of Exodus is that God delivered them out of Egypt.

- Also, there were other people/nations in Egypt, and when they saw what the God of the Israelites did, they went with the Israelites. They saw what God did to the "mighty" Egyptian nation and how God humbled the Egyptian god.

📖 5
page 35
Outline Points B and C

B. Jesus Favored the Poor / C. Jesus Warned against Riches

Highlight the following about these two outline points:

1. Jesus and most biblical characters were the working poor.

2. Jesus chose to live in a working poor situation.

3. Jesus was making a very big statement by showing that you need to value people in poverty.

4. Jesus chose to be a rabbi who didn't have a lot of prestige and didn't command a lot of earthly power. He did so as a model of humility.

5. God can transcend wherever you are as a person, or as a church, as in the Book of Acts.

6. Empowerment is more important than causation.

    • Focus on creating pathways of opportunity.

    • For people who live in the condition of poverty, know that is not their identity, but the condition that they live in.

    • We should respect their talents and abilities and understand that God will utilize them.

📖 **6**
page 37
Student Questions
and Response

Now allow the students to comment on what was presented. Here are some topics that can be discussed if you need to get the discussion going. (NOTE: Don't feel obligated to use them. If your class is going along well, allow the students to discuss freely.)

• World Impact provides effective, affordable, and accessible seminary programs which is a pathway of opportunity. This is directly from the Scriptures.

• The number one reason that pastors don't have formal training is they don't have the money.

• A non-faith-based organization can take some of the principles of redemptive poverty work and do good things; they can make the world a better place. A part of redemptive poverty work is ethical poverty work.

• Discuss working poor in ministry. God has created each of us for a purpose and given us gifts and talents to be able to go out and make the world a better place. So, if we go forth and try to do what we were created to do and expand the Kingdom, there will be provision made for us to have enough.

- Genesis 3 makes it very clear that we live in a fallen world, therefore you will experience hardship in your life. God will utilize those hardships when we engage with others. God will turn your test into a testimony. Trust in God's promises that everything will be all right eventually, even though you may not see it in YOUR lifetime.

- Most people never emerge from poverty.

- The number-one reason why people are in poverty is that they were born into it.

- Or use the following for in-class discussion:

    1. Why are people biblically illiterate?

    2. Besides it being a kingdom priority, what are your top three reasons for pursuing poverty work from a biblical perspective?

    3. Are there legitimate reasons to not pursue it?

📖 7
page 38
Case Study

Discuss the Case Study:

A young urban minister who oversees training volunteers for a tutoring program for a school in an impoverished neighborhood has come to you for advice. Her job is to give an orientation before the volunteers are assigned kids to work with. She has found that she consistently runs into a problem. Every orientation a debate breaks out among the new volunteers concerning the causes of poverty. One group argues that people are poor because they made bad choices in their lives. The others argue that people are poor because of economic injustice. Rarely does either group cite Scripture to back up their arguments. What is your advice to her?

- After some have provided their input, let them know that it does add value to know their backgrounds so we can be informative.

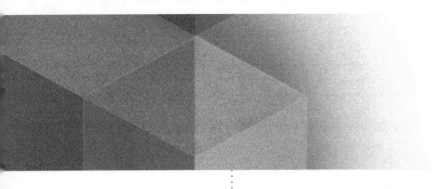

- If you engage people theologically from what the Bible says about poverty, you will address the volunteer's concern.

- Create a pathway of opportunity, regardless of how they got there – love them as God has commanded us to love them, empower them to make their situations better if they desire, and empower them to do that by creative restoration through sacrifice.

LESSON
2

Toxic Poverty Work

📖 **1**
page 41
Lesson Introduction

Welcome to the Mentor's Guide for *Redemptive Poverty Work*, Lesson 2: *Toxic Poverty Work*. This lesson outlines the type of poverty work that naturally arises from our sinful nature. Take some time to clarify this theological point. As image-bearers of Almighty God and followers of Christ, we often seek to do good for those in poverty. However, if we follow our natural impulses with unreflective acts of "service" we often produce *Toxic Poverty Work*. The care and concern of God for the poor can be twisted in ways that are self-serving and destructive.

With this framework in mind, survey the toxic forms our work can take if we do not practice self-awareness. Much of this lesson will recall experiences for your students. You may have people who have done *Toxic Poverty Work* and people who have been the recipients of such work. Allow your students to share and discuss their own experiences of savior syndrome, paternalism, burnout, and cynicism. Healthy poverty work begins when we grapple with the foundational weakness built into our work – the idealistic belief that we can rescue people from their circumstances.

📖 **2**
page 44
Summary

Mindset leads to behaviors, and behaviors affect goals.

1. We come to a situation with certain values, attitudes, and beliefs about said situation or person (our mindset).

2. That will lead to certain behaviors which then affects our goals.

3. For example, an exploitative mindset can lead to toxic behaviors.

4. Genesis 3 tells us that we all sin and fall short of the glory of God. Because of that, if we don't disrupt our thought processes, we're going to do things that may be good coming from our natural selves, but other things we will try to do for selfish reasons.

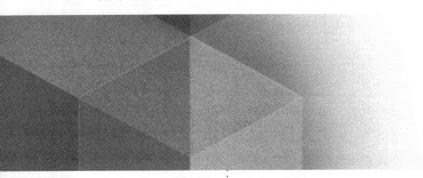

📖 **3**
page 44
Outline Point I

I. Savior Syndrome: Taking on a Role God Never Intended Us to Have

1. We want to go in, save and rescue people and their communities.

2. None of us have the ability to save anybody. We can't save ourselves. We can be used by God to be able to make situations better.

3. We don't have stated intentions to exploit people in poverty, nor do we want to go into a neighborhood and be toxic.

4. Having it brought to your attention that you are not supposed to go out and rescue people, but you're still out there trying to rescue people.

5. If we don't address our ability or our presupposition to go and try to save people, we will end up with a lot of heartache, pain, and suffering. The only thing that people need from us is that Jesus is within us.

📖 **4**
page 45
Outline Point II

II. Paternalism: An Issue of Power Dynamics

1. In offering help, we feel like we are the parent and those in poverty are the child and therefore can't take care of themselves and don't have a voice to engage or give input into their own dreams, hopes, goals, etc.

2. We assume we know what's best.

3. Don't be a dictator. Don't come in, take over, and dictate what is to be done and how it should be done. If we do know what's best, then we should work alongside the individual or the community to find the best way forward with their input and build things together.

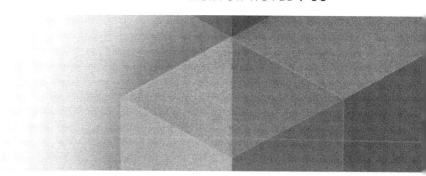

📖 5
page 45
Outline Point III

III. Burnout and Cynicism: Suffering from Fatigue and Disillusionment

Burnout: Suffering from Fatigue

1. Comprised of three things:

   - Having the wrong mindset

   - Continuing to try to save people from their situation

   - Trying to control things all the time (paternalism)

2. Analogous to going 100 miles/hour and not taking care of yourself.

3. A healthy dose of reality that not everything will work out can prevent burnout. We think that what we are doing is going to be miraculous in this community, and when it doesn't happen, it can lead to burnout.

4. We need to take time to reenergize and not be available 24/7. If we are available all the time, something's wrong.

5. Burnout can cause people to leave the church, to question their faith and walk away from the Lord.

Cynicism: Suffering from Disillusionment

1. Essentially, cynicism is when we lose hope. We may feel big doing the work of ministry, but we are cynical about everything and everyone around us; we think that there's no hope for the people or neighborhoods in poverty. Really, we have become heartbroken.

2. It is the cousin of burnout.

3. Everything seems horrible and terrible, like there's no good in the world or in people.

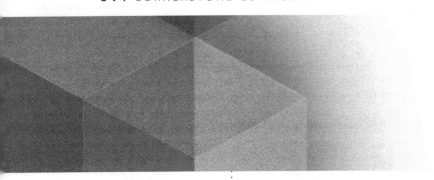

4. Every cynic used to be an idealist.

5. Poverty work can spur us to be cynics because there is so much complexity that we are engaging in when we're dealing with people, especially with those in the condition of poverty.

📖 **6**
page 47
Conclusion

In summary, we've had the wrong mindset when we've gone into situations which led to toxic behaviors which has then led to the wrong goals.

📖 **7**
page 47
Student Questions
and Response

Now allow the students to comment on what was presented. Here are some topics that can be discussed if you need to get the discussion going. (NOTE: Don't feel obligated to use them. If your class is going along well, allow the students to discuss freely.)

*   There may be some people who are ready to receive the truth. With others you simply walk away. Don't argue with them. People typically fall into one of two camps:

    1. Those who want to pretend like they understand, and they want to argue with you all day long.

    2. Those who are trying to figure things out and you can engage (interact with) them.

*   When we help someone and they give their life to Christ, that is just the beginning. We should be prepared with a system or have a strategy in place so that when someone gives their life to Christ, we know the steps that will help us invest in and encourage them to grow in their faith.

*   We should try to model what Jesus did for us in the Scriptures. When Jesus met people at their point of need, he let them know what his motivation was.

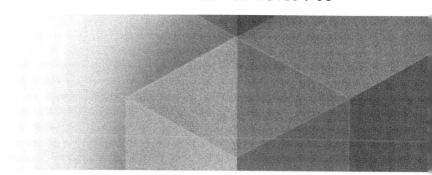

- Or use the following discussion questions:

    1. Have you ever lived in poverty? How does your experience (or lack of it) affect your understanding of poverty?

    2. How easy or hard is it for you to accept that if you have participated in poverty work, at some point, you have practiced toxic poverty work?

    3. What issues do you need to personally engage in after learning of toxic poverty work?

📖 **8**
page 48
Case Study

Discuss the Case Study:

Some friends ask you to visit the Christian food pantry they volunteer at. As someone they trust, they want you to observe and give your opinion on its operations. The first thing you notice as you walk up are some shirtless guys gambling, smoking, and drinking right around the entrance. When you walk in, you are struck by how dark and dingy the interior is. Things seem chaotic and you cannot discern any rhyme or reason to how people receive their groceries. People are getting antsy waiting. Then a young preacher comes into the waiting area and gives a sermon. When he is done, everyone raises their hand to receive Christ. After about an hour, the first person goes forward to get a bag of groceries, which turns into a huge argument between the volunteer and the customer over food choices. The volunteer tells him that he gets whatever is given to him, and he should be happy about it. Afterwards, you go out to lunch with your friends to discuss your observations. What do you tell them?

Let the students respond to this, but here are some suggested items to start off with:

    1. I would go deeper in my observation, into the program itself. What is the intention of the program? Why did they start it?

    2. What is toxic about this situation:

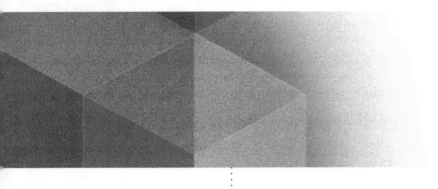

- Front door environment

- Those serving (training needed)

- Esthetics

- Holding people hostage

- Disorganized – the way it is set up creates a lot of problems, instead of bringing solutions or making people feel comfortable when receiving the food.

- Shows that the people coming for help are not being valued.

3. It's important that the people who are being served have ownership. They should believe that what you are doing/providing really benefits them.

4. We should provide assistance with the thought of sustainability. Offer assistance at the request of and alongside the people who are going to be in a community long term, strengthening the program and the calling that God has put on their lives and hearts. That's what will bring lasting change.

Redemptive Poverty Work

 1

page 51
Lesson Introduction

Welcome to the Mentor's Guide for *Redemptive Poverty Work*, Lesson 3: *Redemptive Poverty Work*. This lesson defines the goal of our activity by exploring the three types of poverty work available to us. The first of the three types, the *Exploitative Mindset*, builds directly on the previous discussion of toxic poverty work. In some ways, the exploitative mindset is ignoring the potential for toxicity in poverty work. Help your students make this connection and show them how toxic poverty work and the exploitative mindset go hand-in-hand.

The second mindset, the *Ethical Mindset*, acknowledges the good that anyone can do in society. Not every action of poverty workers will be toxic or have destructive consequences. Even apart from a redemptive model, people often work for the common good in ethical ways. Help your students to think of organizations and people that do ethical poverty work. Such organizations and people can be legitimate and helpful partners for us as we do redemptive poverty work.

The third mindset, *Redemptive Poverty Work*, imitates the work that Christ has done on the cross as we pursue redemption of lives and neighborhoods. It is crucial that your students see the connection between Christ's own redemptive work and the work we seek to do. *Redemptive Poverty Work* is not a new strategy or an innovative idea. It is simply modeling our poverty work after Christ's own self-sacrificial redemptive work. There can be no more reliable methodology than what God has employed in Christ.

📖 2
page 54
Outline Point I

I. Three Distinct Mindsets When It Comes to How We Approach Poverty Work

There are three types of work that happens within the world that you read about or saw in the video.

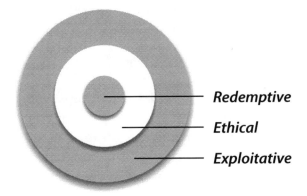

Redemptive

Ethical

Exploitative

A. The outer layer of our self-awareness is the *Exploitative Mindset* of Poverty Work.

1. Leads to the savior syndrome mentality

2. I am here to rescue you and your neighborhood.

3. It's all about me.

4. It's not intentional, but it happens because we're not conscious of ourselves and how we're moving in a particular person's life or in a particular community.

5. You're trying to get something out of someone or out of a community.

6. The question becomes, "Do we ever mature and realize that I am not here for me, that I am here to represent God? The people in this community don't need me, they need the Jesus in me. They need to know the Good News."

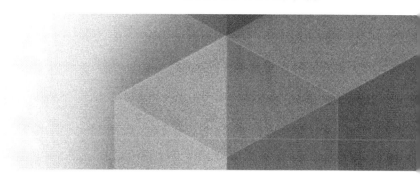

B. The next level up in our self-awareness is the *Ethical Mindset* of Poverty Work.

1. This is the highest level one can achieve without knowing Christ.

2. Nothing wrong with ethical poverty work

3. You have evolved beyond; from "I am here for me" to "I'm actually here for these people."

4. It's a win-win mentality. "I want to win, you want to win, so let's work together and collaborate so that everyone wins in this situation."

5. Ethical Poverty Work is the foundation of what God is calling World Impact to do, which is Redemptive Poverty Work.

C. Finally, there is the *Redemptive Mindset* of Poverty Work.

1. Creative restoration through sacrifice

2. It has everything to do with motive and the rate of restoration through sacrifice. It's following the pattern that Christ followed to redeem us.

3. Motivated to sacrifice our time and treasures because Christ did the same for us

4. We are not the savior of this community (we are working in) but Christ is the Savior. We want to introduce them to the ways of Christ so that they may be able to take a pathway of opportunity when it comes to them being in poverty.

3

REDEMPTIVE POVERTY WORK

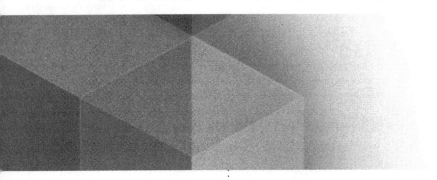

📖 3

page 55
Outline Point II

II. Redemptive Work in the Bible

Characteristics of Redemptive Poverty Work:

- Ethical empowerment

- Creative restoration through sacrifice

- God is bigger than the circumstances.

- Poverty is a condition, not an identity.

- Walk by faith while rearranging human systemic power.

1. Ethical empowerment

    - I sacrifice, you win. It matters how we do things. It matters how people respond.

    - It's not just about us, it's not just about them, it's about working together collaboratively so that God can receive and get all the glory.

2. Creative restoration through sacrifice

    - The pattern that Christ used to redeem us.

    - Because of what Jesus has done for us, we want to do so for others.

    - You are doing this and trying to work to make the situation better for people who live in a condition of poverty whether it benefits you or not. You are going to sacrifice and try to make their lives better, just like what Christ has done for the entire world.

3. God is bigger than the circumstances.

    - This is obvious but easily forgettable.

    - God is bigger than the circumstances that we see, and God is big in spite of the circumstances.

- When we look at situations – people's lives and neighborhoods – we always have faith that God can overcome this and that God can use me to make a difference in that situation.

📖 4
page 55
Outline Point III

Our Role as Redemptive Poverty Workers

Poverty is a condition, not an identity.

1. The big mistake of society is that our social class standing becomes our identity. It has a big influence on us.

2. We should engage that, and not allow our social status to become ALL of our identity.

3. Especially for those in poverty, their existence from a societal standpoint is put on a lower level of humanity because they don't have a lot of financial resources. Most do not want to live in their neighborhood.

4. God uses people whether we are wealthy, or have no money at all, or are somewhere in between.

5. And as a side note – racial identity is tied up in all of this as well. You may not know where race begins, and social class ends. They really don't. They are tied up in one big ball together, so that if you are black or brown, it's assumed that you're poor or live in poverty or know about poverty.

6. Our proper lens is to view people in poverty the same way we would view anybody else and not assign negative connotations to them. God has given them the same gifting and talents he has given everybody else. The Kingdom of God is moving amongst them through the power of the local church.

7. In Ephesians, the Apostle Paul understood that his identity was not in whatever condition he found himself in, but that his identity was always in being a child of God and follower of Jesus Christ.

3

REDEMPTIVE POVERTY WORK

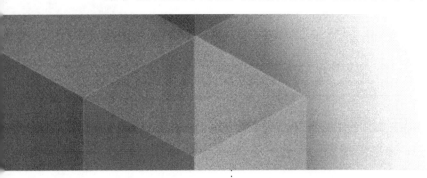

8. Because Christ is with us, that is what we put our faith, hope, and trust in.

Walk by faith while rearranging human systemic power.

1. Our advocacy and going into social justice situations are with the eye of God. We want God to move in these situations.

2. We are motivated by theological principles. Social and cultural principles enhance those theological principles. You can tie in the social and the cultural landscape after the theological foundation has been laid.

3. When we engage those forces that are trying to make people less than human and trying to make communities less than what their true potential is . . . we know that what we're doing is by faith in God. Regardless of the outcome, it does not change the fact that we are always striving to make this world a better place.

📖 **5**
page 56
*Student Questions
and Response*

Now allow the students to comment on what was presented. Here are some topics that can be discussed if you need to get the discussion going. (NOTE: Don't feel obligated to use them. If your class is going along well, allow the students to discuss freely.)

*   The Church needs to define where it fits in with the social upheavals and shifting. When it comes to social issues taking place all over the world, oftentimes, the Church is very silent. They don't want to get involved in political matters or believe these are political matters and should not be engaged by the Church.

*   Because the churches are silent, many young people are looking for places and spaces where they can find advocacy.

*   Is it possible for a church to work alongside an organization that is not ethical or exploits people if it's for the common good?

*   Lead with the Word and then tell the truth about social conditions that exist.

- On an institutional level, confront injustice. On a personal level, the Bible tells us to create pathways of opportunity for people who are in the condition of poverty to live a more humane life and to switch social classes. But some/many may not switch social classes. It is important to know that Jesus is with us even in the midst of our suffering.

- Or use the following discussion questions:

  1. How has redemption changed your personal life?

  2. Does the notion of redemptive poverty work resonate with you? Explain why or why not.

  3. What is the main difference between *ethical* and *redemptive* poverty work?

📖 6

page 57
Case Study

Discuss the Case Study:

You have been working with Sheri for five years. By all accounts, Sheri is a good woman with a rock-solid faith. She attends church every Sunday that she is not scheduled to work at a hotel as a maid. She brings home just enough money to make ends meet for her and her three children, as their father does not contribute much to their lives. Right now, she is upset because she just found out that one of her sons has been expelled from a private Christian school that you played a key role in getting him admitted to. On one hand, she is embarrassed; on the other, she feels invisible to God because in her opinion the school is over-reacting because of his race and social class. What is your response to her?

Let the students respond to this, but here are some suggested items to start off with:

- Since I took part in getting the young man in the school, I would feel a responsibility to talk to the administration to hear their side of the story and then hear from the young man.

- Since it states in the case study that the father doesn't play a part in the kids' life, I would see if there is a man in the church that

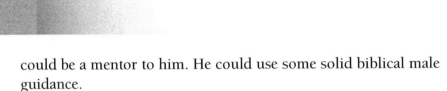

could be a mentor to him. He could use some solid biblical male guidance.

- At the end of the discussion, explain the reason for the expulsion and see if that changes anyone's opinion: The young man wore one of his older brother's T-shirts that had a marijuana leaf on it. From the culture in which he grew up in, there was nothing to it. He wasn't doing or selling drugs. The school felt it was aggressive and instead of talking it out to see what could be learned from a cultural perspective from both sides, they stated that they don't advocate drugs and ruled his behavior sinful and wrong and expelled him. The school is killing a fly with a sledgehammer.

Rhythms of Life and Poverty Work

📖 **1**

page 61

Lesson Introduction

Welcome to the Mentor's Guide for *Redemptive Poverty Work*, Lesson 4: *Rhythms of Life and Poverty Work*. This lesson lays out spiritual practices for poverty work that are connected to the Great Tradition of the Church.

It is essential that you help your students understand what is meant by *The Great Tradition*. Here is a good working definition: "The Great Tradition represents the central core of Christian belief and practice derived from Scripture that runs between the time of Christ and the middle of the fifth century" (Dr. Don Davis, *Sacred Roots*, TUMI: 2010, p. 74).

Here is a helpful expansion on this definition: "It is the legacy of early Christian engagement with Scripture that fundamentally shaped the Church as we know it. The early church built a rule of faith (a creed) that summarizes the core of the faith from Scripture. They created a service of the Word and the Table that keys all gathered worship to the Gospel of Christ and his Kingdom. They Christianized the Jewish festival calendar to pattern their own spiritual lives on the story of God in Christ. The Word of God dwelt richly in them and they became a light representing Christ and his Kingdom in the world. Their beliefs and practices became the Sacred Roots of every branch of the church" (Ryan Carter, *Guard the Good Deposit*, TUMI: 2019, pp. 11-12).

Poverty work has been essential to the Church from her earliest days. The Great Tradition developed not apart from poverty but in the midst of it. In fact, many early Christians were from the poor, low, and despised classes of society. The contention of this lesson is that Redemptive Poverty Work cannot be separated from the beliefs and practices of Great Tradition. It is critical that you help your students maintain the proper link in their mind between who we are as the Church and what we do in the world. If we truly hope to see people and neighborhoods redeemed, our work must flow from and build to a robust church life rooted in the Great Tradition.

The spiritual practices outlined in this lesson are designed to help you and your students embrace and embody in this conviction. They are practical ways for us to enact our shared life, shared journey, shared discipline and shared confession.

📖 **2**
page 63
Summary

In working in communities of poverty and serving those whose lives are being taxed by spiritual, physical, or psychological trauma, it's going to be a challenge to maintain the freshness and strength that you need. You can get that freshness and strength from these Rhythms of Life. They can safeguard us from being burned out, being toxic ourselves, and from being overly stressed.

Three months living and working in communities that are stressed and economically deprived and socially under the gun is enough to break all altruism that you started with.

People called to serve in these communities often think that because God has called them to poverty work, they will be fine. What they discover is that their own personal lives, their minds, their bodies, the lack of sleep, the long hours, all the things that come with ministering in these communities are affected. They find that they themselves are the object of the devil's attack.

You can't give to others what you do not personally own. "You can't give what you ain't got, and you can't lose what you ain't never had" (Muddy Waters). So the first thing above everything else in doing ministry in at-risk neighborhoods is your own soul care.

📖 **3**
page 65
Outline Point B, 1

Church Membership

- Commit to active membership within a healthy local church for the purposes of fellowship, teaching, prayer, service, and personal development.

- Being a part of a church community allows you to receive pastoral care, good feeding/teaching, fellowship, and blessings.

- It is critical to *Redemptive Poverty Work* because the main redemptive institution for the world, that we see from the Bible's teachings, is the local church.

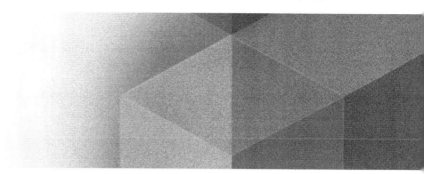

- The church is a vibrant institution that is supposed to be the group of people who have been called to redeem the world to do the things that they need to keep themselves connected to God.

📖 4
page 66
Outline Point B, 2

Fixed Times of Prayer

- Prayer allows us to stop seeing circumstances as bigger than God, but that God is bigger than the circumstances.

- We should set focused time to pray to the Lord once or twice a day either in a group or by ourselves.

- It can be seen as an interruption of your day, but it's not really disrupting your day to remind yourself that you belong to God.

📖 5
page 66
Outline Point B, 3

Empowerment

- We are not trying to increase our own personal influence and profile or the organization's influence and profile on the backs of those we claim to serve.

- Instead of seeking to increase our personal profile, we work to empower others.

- Our ministry partners are the heroes. That's why we feature them and not World Impact staff in World Impact videos. We want people to see our partners empowered to do the work of the Lord.

📖 6
page 67
Outline Point B, 4

Church Calendar

- Instead of viewing time only chronologically, we sanctify time by connecting our story to the story of God through the Church Year Calendar.

- This is a Christ-oriented way of understanding every day.

REDEMPTIVE POVERTY WORK

4

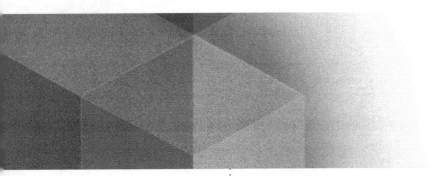

- Using the Church Year Calendar helps us to remember that, regardless of what may be happening in our lives and our hearts chronologically, we want to remember God's story by attaching our personal lives, our personal ministry to the story of God.

📖 7
page 67
Outline Point B, 5

Sabbath

- Instead of constant advocacy, we follow a pattern of work and rest.

- This is often violated amongst people who do ministry in communities of poverty.

📖 8
page 68
Outline Point B, 6

Personal Retreat

- Instead of a life of busyness and distraction, we take time to orient our lives towards obedience to God.

- Suggestion: take a workday once a month to reflect on your life, reflect on your work, look back at what's happened in the last month and plan for the coming month.

📖 9
page 68
Outline Point B, 7

Tithing

- Instead of anxiety about money, or worship of money, we generously give.

- Figure out what you should be giving and give it away to entities that help the economically poor.

- Make it a part of your own personal discipline to give of your own resources to the work of the Lord.

4

REDEMPTIVE POVERTY WORK

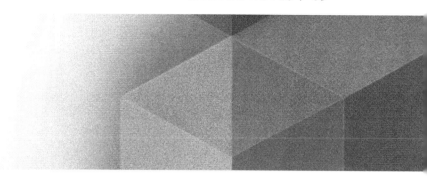

📖 **10**
page 69
Outline Point B, 8

Fasting

- Instead of seeking control, we fast in response to situations in life.

- Fasting from a biblical perspective is to get closer to God. And because you are closer to God, no matter what happens you will be able to handle it.

- It has to be disciplined within the framework of your own health.

📖 **11**
page 69
Conclusion

If you do all or most of the disciplines, it is impossible to ignore God. You can't get too far away from God if you are constantly doing things to remind yourself that you are supposed to be connected to God.

These are the eight disciplines that the Great Tradition (which all TUMI materials are based upon) displays.

📖 **12**
page 70
Student Questions
and Response

Now allow the students to comment on what was presented. Here are some topics that can be discussed if you need to get the discussion going. (NOTE: Don't feel obligated to use them. If your class is going along well, allow the students to discuss freely.)

- Ask the class how they have been challenged to have personal time/vacation.

- Ask the class about their own physical habits of care: do they get enough sleep, are they eating well, are they exercising, are they drinking enough water, etc.?

- It was suggested to a group of community pastors who lived in a house in the neighborhood that they put a sign on the door: "Closed on Mondays" because they were constantly (daily, hourly) being asked for something. They thought the idea was demonic and unlike Jesus. You will actually teach them what your boundaries are, and they might, in return, actually learn some boundaries as well.

4

REDEMPTIVE POVERTY WORK

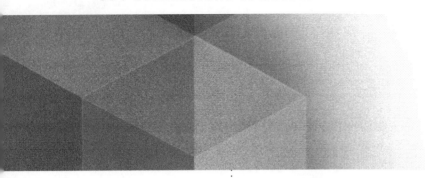

- After fourteen years as missionaries where people were always asking for something (every hour, hundreds of people being cared for by two), one of the two missionaries was having physical symptoms that were diagnosed as stress. They found out that vacations and retreats are very important.

- Or use the following discussion questions:

    1. Why is it important that advocacy is grounded in spiritual practices?

    2. In what practical ways have you tied your advocacy to your faith?

    3. How many of the spiritual practices do you engage in on a regular basis?

📖 **13**
page 71
Case Study

Discuss the Case Study:

You do poverty work in an urban neighborhood and run into a colleague at the corner store. He asks if you have some time to spare to talk. After walking to his office and starting to talk, it is apparent he is angry and frustrated. He is overwhelmed by the challenges he faces daily. The challenges don't shock you because you face the same ones. However, what does shock you is his tone and what he is saying. He is very cynical about the people in the neighborhood and the organizations set up to help them, including the local church he belongs to which he has stopped attending. His complaints revolve around not being appreciated for the sacrifices he has made and how physically tired he is. What would you tell him?

Let the students respond to this, but here are some suggested items to start off with:

- Allow him to vent and air out his issues. Then suggest that he can get some time off to spend time with the Lord. He seems to be disconnected from God.

- Encourage him to get back to fellowship in a church.

- One of the easiest things to do in ministry, especially if you're in a pastoral or supervisory role, is to think that you don't need a pastor.

📖 **14**
page 72
Other Assignments

Quizzes and answer keys for each lesson can be found online at World Impact U in the Redemptive Poverty Work Dashboard. (These are available to the Partner and Mentor.)

- Quiz 1: Lesson 1: A Brief Theological Reflection

- Quiz 2: Lesson 2: Toxic Poverty Work

- Quiz 3: Lesson 3: Redemptive Poverty Work

- Final Exam (includes questions from Lesson 4: Rhythms of Life and Poverty Work)

- Answer Key

After your students complete the Final Exam, please direct them to the *Redemptive Poverty Work Course Survey*. While we prefer this form be completed online, circumstances may prevent this from being possible. The form is included in the Appendix section of this book. Please scan the completed forms and send to the *Redemptive Poverty Work* representative.

- *Redemptive Poverty Work Course Survey* URL: https://tinyurl.com/d34tmhkv

- *Redemptive Poverty Work Course Survey* (see Appendix)

4

REDEMPTIVE POVERTY WORK

Parts II and III

Cornerstone Curriculum

Mentoring Parts II and III:
The Cornerstone Curriculum

Before the Course Begins

- First, read carefully the Introduction found on page 9, and browse through the Student Workbook and Mentor's Guide in order to gain an understanding of the content that will be covered. The Student Workbook contains all of the lessons and assignments, as well as references (indicated by a symbol in the margin: 📖) to additional *Mentor's Notes* which can be found in this volume. Each note is cross-referenced with page numbers to help you move back and forth between the Student Workbook and the Mentor's Guide. The Unit Exams and Answer Key can be found on the WIU Dashboard.

- Second, you are strongly encouraged to view the teaching on both DVDs prior to the beginning of the course.

- Third, you should read any assigned readings associated with the curriculum, whether textbooks, articles or appendices.

- Fourth, it may be helpful to review the key theological themes associated with the course by using Bible dictionaries, theological dictionaries, and commentaries to refresh your familiarity with major topics covered in the curriculum.

- Fifth, please know that the students *are not tested on the reading assignments*. These are given to help the students get a fuller understanding of what the lesson is teaching, but it is not required that your students be excellent readers to understand what is being taught. For those of you who are receiving this curriculum in any translation other than English, the required reading might not be available in your language. Please select a book or two that is available in your language – one that you think best represents what is being taught in this curriculum – and assign that to your students instead.

- Finally, begin to think about key questions and areas of ministry training that you would like to explore with students in light of the content that is being covered.

Before Each Lesson

Prior to each lesson, you should once again watch the teaching content that is found on the DVD for that class session, and then create a *Contact* and *Connection* section for this lesson.

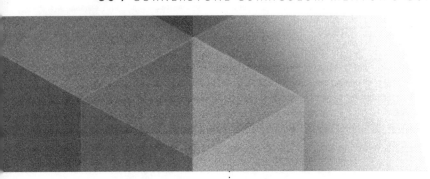

Preparing the Contact Section

Review the Mentor's Guide to understand the lesson objectives and gather ideas for possible Contact activities. (Two to three Contacts are provided which you may use, or feel free to create your own, if that is more appropriate.)

Then, create a Contact section that introduces the students to the lesson content and captures their interest. As a rule, Contact methods fall into three general categories.

Attention Focusers capture student attention and introduce them to the lesson topic. Attention focusers can be used by themselves with motivated learners or combined with one of the other methods described below. Examples:

- Singing an opening song related to the lesson theme.

- Showing a cartoon or telling a joke that relates to an issue addressed by the lesson.

- Asking students to stand on the left side of the room if they believe that it is easier to teach people how to be saved from the Gospels and to stand on the right side if they believe it is easier to teach people from the Epistles.

Storytelling methods either have the instructor tell a story that illustrates the importance of the lesson content or ask students to share their experiences (stories) about the topic that will be discussed. Examples:

- In a lesson on the role of the pastor, a Mentor may tell the story of conducting a funeral and share the questions and challenges that were part of the experience.

- In a lesson about evangelism, the Mentor may ask students to describe an experience they have had of sharing the Gospel.

Problem-posing activities raise challenging questions for students to answer and lead them toward the lesson content as a source for answering those questions, or they may ask students to list the unanswered questions that they have about the topic that will be discussed. Examples:

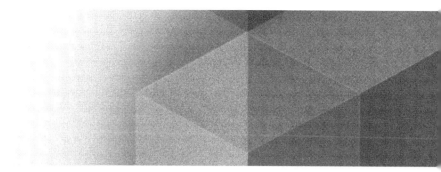

- Presenting case studies from ministry situations that call for a leadership decision and having students discuss what the best response would be.

- Problems framed as questions such as "When preaching at a funeral, is it more important for a minister to be truthful or compassionate? Why?"

Regardless of what method is chosen, the key to a successful Contact section is making a transition from the Contact to the Content of the lesson. When planning the Contact section, Mentors should write out a transition statement that builds a bridge from the Contact to the lesson content. For example, if the lesson content was on the truth that the Holy Spirit is a divine Person who is a full member of the Godhead, the Contact activity might be to have students quickly draw a symbol that best represents the Holy Spirit to them. After having them share their drawings and discuss why they chose what they did, the Mentor might make a transition statement along the following lines:

> Because the Holy Spirit is often represented by symbols like fire or oil in Scripture rather than with a human image like the Father or the Son, it is sometimes difficult to help people understand that the Spirit is a full person within the Godhead who thinks, acts, and speaks as personally as God the Father or Jesus Christ. In this lesson, we want to establish the scriptural basis for understanding that the Spirit is more than just a symbol for "God's power" and think about ways that we can make this plain to people in our congregations.

This is a helpful transition statement because it directs the students to what they can expect from the lesson content and also prepares them for some of the things that might be discussed in the Connection section that comes later. Although you may adapt your transition statement based on student responses during the Contact section, it is important, during the planning time, to think about what will be said.

Three useful questions for evaluating the Contact section you have created are:

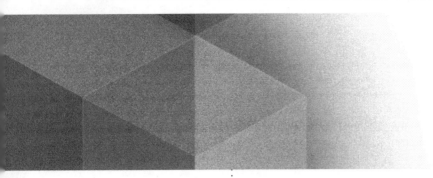

- Is it creative and interesting?

- Does it take into account the needs and interests of this particular group?

- Does it focus people toward the lesson content and arouse their interest in it?

Preparing the Connection Section

Again, review the Mentor's Guide to understand the lesson objectives and gather ideas for possible Connection activities.

Then, create a Connection section that helps students form new associations between truth and their lives (implications) and discuss specific changes in their beliefs, attitudes, or actions that should occur as a result (applications). As you plan, be a little wary of making the Connection section overly specific. Generally this lesson section should come to students as an invitation to discover, rather than as a finished product with all the specific outcomes predetermined.

At the heart of every good Connection section is a question (or series of questions) that asks students how knowing the truth will change their thinking, attitudes, and behaviors. (We have included some Connection questions in order to "prime the pump" of your students, to spur their thinking, and help them generate their own questions arising from their life experience.) Because this is theological and ministry training, the changes we are most concerned with are those associated with the way in which the students train and lead others in their ministry context. Try and focus in on helping students think about this area of application in the questions you develop.

The Connection section can utilize a number of different formats. Students can discuss the implications and applications together in a large Mentor-led group or in small groups with other students (either open discussion or following a pre-written set of questions). Case studies, also, are often good discussion starters. Regardless of the method, in this section both the Mentor and the learning group

itself should be seen as a source of wisdom. Since your students are themselves already Christian leaders, there is often a wealth of experience and knowledge that can be drawn on from the students themselves. Students should be encouraged to learn from each other as well as from the Mentor.

Several principles should guide the Connection discussions that you lead:

- First, the primary goal in this section is to bring to the surface the questions that students have. In other words, the questions that occur to students during the lesson take priority over any questions that the Mentor prepares in advance – although the questions raised by an experienced Mentor will still be a useful learning tool. A corollary to this is to assume that the question raised by one student is very often the unspoken question present among the entire group.

- Second, try and focus the discussion on the concrete and the specific rather than the purely theoretical or hypothetical. This part of the lesson is meant to focus on the actual situations that are being faced by the specific students in your classroom.

- Third, do not be afraid to share the wisdom that you have gained through your own ministry experience. You are a key resource to students and they should expect that you will make lessons you have learned available to them. However, always keep in mind that variables of culture, context, and personality may mean that what has worked for you may not always work for everyone. Make suggestions, but dialogue with students about whether your experience seems workable in their context, and if not, what adaptations might be made to make it so.

Three useful questions for evaluating the Connection section you have created are:

- Have I anticipated in advance what the general areas of implication and application are likely to be for the teaching that is given in the lesson?

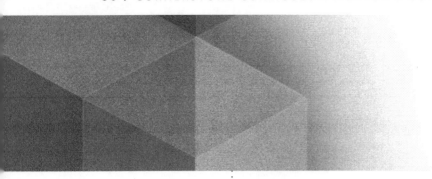

- Have I created a way to bring student questions to the surface and give them priority?

- Will this help a student leave the classroom knowing what to do with the truth they have learned?

Finally, because the Ministry Project is the structured application project for the entire course, it will be helpful to set aside part of the Connection section to have students discuss what they might choose for their project and to evaluate progress and/or report to the class following completion of the assignment.

Steps in Leading a Lesson

Opening Activities

- Take attendance.

- Lead the devotion.

- Say or sing the Nicene Creed and pray.

- Check Scripture memorization assignment.

- Collect any assignments that are due.

Teach the Contact Section

- Use a Contact provided in the Mentor's Guide, or create your own.

Oversee the Content Section

- Present the Content of the lesson using the video teaching.

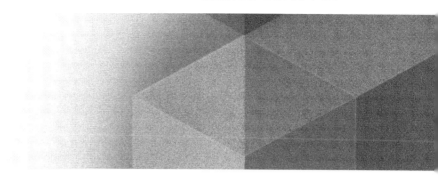

Using the Videos

Each lesson has one video teaching, approximately 25 minutes in length. After teaching the Contact section (including the transition statement), play the video for the students. Students can follow this presentation using their Student Workbook which contains a general outline of the material presented and Scripture references and other supplementary materials referenced by the speaker. Once the video is viewed, work with the students to confirm that the content was understood.

Ensuring That the Content Is Understood

Using the Mentor's Guide, check for comprehension by asking the questions listed in the "Student Questions and Response" section. Clarify any incomplete understandings that students may demonstrate in their answers.

Ask students if there are any questions that they have about the content and discuss them together as a class. NOTE: The questions here should focus on understanding the content itself rather than on how to apply the learning. Application questions will be the focus of the upcoming Connection section.

Teach the Connection Section

- Summary of Key Concepts
- Student Application and Implications
- Case Studies
- Restatement of Lesson's Thesis
- Resources and Bibliographies

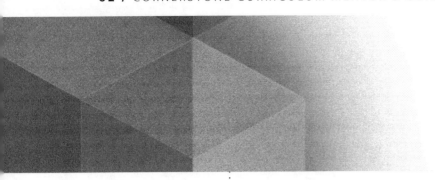

- Ministry Connections

- Counseling and Prayer

Remind Students of Upcoming Assignments

- Scripture Memorization

- Assigned Readings

- Other Assignments

Close Lesson

- Close with prayer.

- Be available for any individual student's questions or needs following the class.

Please see the following "Lesson Outline."

Lesson Outline

Introduction

Lesson Title

Lesson Objectives

Devotion

Nicene Creed and Prayer

Scripture Memorization Review

Assignments Due

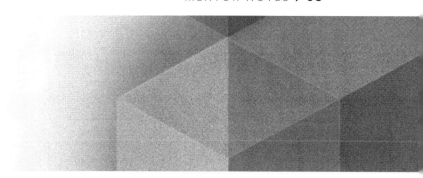

Contact

Contact (1-3)

Content

Video Outline

Student Questions and Response

Connection

Summary of Key Concepts

Student Application and Implications

Case Studies

Restatement of Lesson's Thesis

Resources and Bibliographies

Ministry Connections

Counseling and Prayer

Assignments

Scripture Memorization

Reading Assignment

Other Assignments

Looking Forward to the Next Lesson

Part II

Bible &
Theology

BIBLE &
THEOLOGY
UNIT 1

Biblical
Studies

LESSON
1

Conversion and Calling
The Word That Creates

📖 **1**
page 81
Lesson Introduction

Welcome to the Mentor's Guide for Lesson 1, *Conversion and Calling: The Word That Creates*. The overall focus of this lesson is to enable urban Christian workers and leaders to appreciate, affirm, and apply the Scriptures to every facet of their lives and ministries. Above all other sources, materials, and tools that the man or woman of God employs to represent Christ and his Kingdom, nothing is more critical than the Word of God as the premier and final standard of truth and practice for Christian discipleship. Your task in this lesson is to help your students discover the power of Scripture, especially in its role to convert the Christian and confirm the calling of God in the leader's life. Notice that every lesson has stated learning objectives, and these aims are meant to serve as guides for you throughout the lesson; they are clearly stated, and you ought to emphasize them throughout the lesson, and refer to them especially during the discussions and interaction with the students. The more you can highlight the objectives throughout the class period, the better the chances will be that the students come to understand and grasp the magnitude of these objectives. For this lesson, you will focus on the nature of the Word of God to create new life. Concentrate on this creative aspect throughout your leading of the lesson.

📖 **2**
page 81
Lesson Objectives

Again, make certain that you gear your class session explicitly around these objectives, calling attention to them briefly before you enter into the class period. Draw the students attention to the objectives, for, in a real sense, this is the heart of your educational aim for the class period in this lesson. Everything discussed and done ought to point back to these objectives. Find ways to highlight these at every turn, to reinforce them and reiterate them as you go.

📖 **3**
page 81
Devotion

Perhaps one of the most difficult issues you will have to face in your students is the tendency to take the Word of God for granted. Those who minister tend to ignore the pleasure and power of the Word of God for their own lives; in their haste to minister and work with and for others, they can find themselves dry and spent, without proper spiritual nourishment and enlightenment. This devotion focuses on

BIBLICAL STUDIES **1**

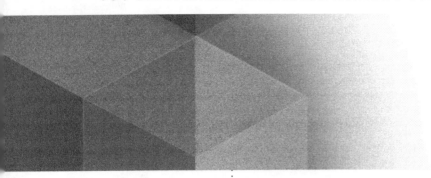

1

BIBLICAL STUDIES

the unbelievable treasure that the Word of God is, and challenges us to concentrate on it first as our very own food and life source, then as the indispensable weapon it is in ministry. For all facets of life and ministry, nothing provides power, encouragement, and refreshment like the Word of God.

📖 **4**
page 82
Nicene Creed
and Prayer

These prayers ought not to be seen as simply a part of the lesson but as a historical and spiritual indicator of the longing we have that God empowers us to know and apply his Word. Only God through the Spirit can enable us to properly view and value his holy Word. Encourage students to depend on the Lord to help them understand the power of the Word that creates.

📖 **5**
page 83
Contact

These contacts seek to create a context by which the students can begin to hear the presentations that follow. These contacts are designed to help the students come to reflect on the role of the Word of God in various situations, its importance and significance, and its role in addressing issues and solving problems. Use these contacts to help the students discuss the role of Scripture in various contexts meaningful in society and in their lives.

📖 **6**
page 91
Student Questions
and Response

The creative power of the Word of God is seen concretely and spiritually in this lesson, and your discussion ought to highlight this powerful aspect of the Scriptures. The fact that the Word of God has special power in God's creative act is perhaps best summarized in Psalm 147.15-20:

> He sends forth his command to the earth; his word runs very swiftly. [16] He gives snow like wool; he scatters the frost like ashes. [17] He casts forth his ice as fragments; Who can stand before his cold? [18] He sends forth his word and melts them; he causes his wind to blow and the waters to flow. [19] He declares his words to Jacob, his statutes and his ordinances to Israel. [20] He has not dealt thus with any nation; And as for his ordinances, they have not known them. Praise the LORD!

This text highlights the principle that ought to be thoroughly discussed and understood during your question and response time.

📖 **7**
page 91
Summary of
Key Concepts

Listed in this section are the fundamental truths written in sentence form which the students should have received from this lesson, that is, from the videos and your guided discussion with them. Do not hesitate to repeat concepts or truths for emphasis. Make sure that these concepts are clearly defined and carefully considered, for their quiz work and exams will be taken from these items directly. More importantly, seek to use the time well so you know that the students understand these fundamental ideas which define this lesson.

📖 **8**
page 92
Student Application
and Implications

In helping your students think through their own situations, you might want to design some questions or use those provided below as water to "prime the pump" of their interests, so to speak. What is significant here is not the questions written below, but for you, in conversation with your students, to settle on a cadre of issues, concerns, questions, and ideas that flow directly from their experience, and relate to their lives and ministries. What we are seeking here is the addressing of the critical concerns the students generate from their own questions and concerns, especially those that they consider most relevant in their ministry context right now. The goal of this section is for you to enable them to think critically and theologically in regards to their own lives and ministry contexts. Again, the questions below are provided as guides and primers, and ought not to be seen as absolute necessities. Pick and choose among them, or come up with your own. The key is relevance now, so be extremely open to them defining the issues and determining the questions that you answer now.

📖 **9**
page 93
Case Studies

The nature of case studies is to allow the students to creatively apply the truths that they have been discussing to real or imagined situations. There are technically no correct answers in the sense that only one way can be determined to handle or comprehend them. What you seek

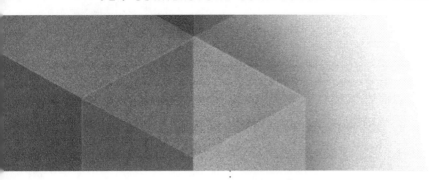

through your consideration of these is the students' ability to connect their learning with realistic ministry situations that will demand their diagnosis, treatment, and prognosis of spiritual issues and problems. In a real sense, case studies are about creative problem solving, so help the students seek to connect their learning to the central issues that run through the situation. Have the students isolate the issues that need to be resolved, and articulate the biblical principles associated with their views. Help them to articulate their positions clearly, and encourage interaction with the students and the facts of the studies.

📖 **10**
page 95
Ministry Connections

Every lesson allows for each student to consider how the particular truths of the lesson relates and applies to their particular lives and ministries. Undoubtedly, the principles you cover relate to the lives of the students, and if you know how, you may emphasize them, or help the students to see the connections, and respond appropriately if they can. Application of the Word of God to their individual lives is the goal of this section. Encourage the students to reflect on their personal lives to see how the Holy Spirit might want them to apply these truths in their lives this week.

📖 **11**
page 95
Counseling and Prayer

Be available, if time permits, for specific counseling and prayer your students might have in their lives and ministries. The goal of all theological and missiological education is to enable individual students to make the Word of God come alive in their personal lives and through them in their assemblies and the ministries that flow from them. Your personal knowledge of the students, and their openness to you ought to provide some degree of counseling for you with them. Do not force it with your students, but be open to it, and expect it. The Scriptures will open up your students to God and his plan, so your readiness to help specifically and concretely is a pivotal part of your mentoring responsibility with them. Remind the students that the Word of God is for application, not merely reflection and discussion (James 1.22-25). Let the Holy Spirit lead you as you listen and respond to your students.

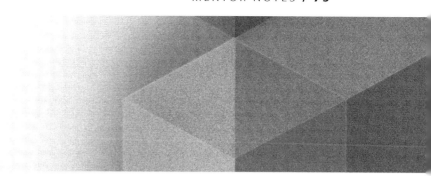

📖 **12**
page 96
Assignments

Administration of the details of the course, along with record-keeping and good communication, are a central part of your role as mentor. Along these lines, it is necessary that you make certain that the students understand the assignment for next week, especially the written piece. This is not difficult; the goal is that they would read the material as best as they can and write a few sentences on what they take them to mean. This is a critical intellectual skill for your students to learn, so make sure that you encourage them in this process. Of course, for those students whose skills make this burdensome and/or difficult, assure them that the intent of this assignment is to encourage them to understand the material, and not to show off their writing skills. While the improvement of writing skills is a worthy goal, we do not want to emphasize such skills at the expense of their encouragement and edification. Nor, however, do we want to sell them short. Strike to find the midpoint between challenge and encouragement here.

1

BIBLICAL STUDIES

Bible Interpretation
The Three-Step Model

📖 **1**
page 99
Lesson Introduction

Welcome to the Mentor's Guide for Lesson 2, *Bible Interpretation: The Three-Step Model*. The overall focus of this lesson is to provide the students with an effective, workable, and time honored approach to biblical interpretation that will allow them to grow in their skills of exegesis. You will introduce the students to the fundamental principles underlying a critical approach to the Bible, but not an approach which either encourages skepticism or over-reliance on scientific methods and approaches. As mentioned in the previous lesson, apart from the illuminating work of the Holy Spirit, no biblical interpreter can possibly understand the mind and thoughts of God on any subject, let alone his divine purpose for salvation in Christ Jesus (1 Cor. 2.9-16). We do, however, require an approach to Scripture that is neither haphazard nor arbitrary. *The Three-Step Model* is designed to help your students come to grips with their need for such an approach, and become effective at using it.

In some ways, this model is not new, but is an extension and expansion of the most basic principles in the interpretation of Scripture recognized by evangelical scholars for many years. The first principle is the importance of *literal interpretation*, which essentially means that the words and sentences of the Bible ought to be understood, first of all, in their *normal sense*, unless of course, such a sense does not make any sense! With the help of philological and linguistic aids, our goal is to read the Bible like any other book of literature, that is, that we seek to understand the words as they are understood in normal communication. The *Three-Step Model* takes seriously the power of language as God's vehicle to communicate with us through his Son and the Holy Spirit, and it affirms the precedence within the Scriptures itself that OT prophecies were interpreted as *literally true* in passages such as Psalms 22, Isaiah 7.14, and Micah 5.2.

You will notice, too, that the structure and nature of language is taken seriously by the *Three-Step Model*, in other words, it pays close attention to the *grammatical relationships between the terms of a text*, and how the actual words function syntactically in relationship to one another. The model affirms the "verbal plenary" understanding of inspiration, which asserts that both the words (verbal) and the entirety of Scripture (plenary) are fully inspired by the Holy Spirit, and as such we must attend to the precise wording of the text as well as the whole of it. The

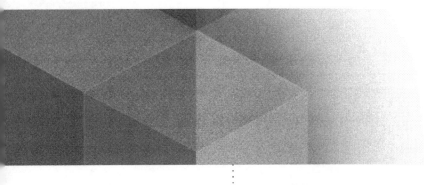

essential rules of language and literature all apply to the grammatical relationships of the text, and so it will be important to pay close attention to the words and the rules which connect them together.

Since the *Three-Step Model* focuses on the importance of bridging the gap between the world of the text and our contemporary world, it is structured around the need to understand the text in its original situation, i.e., its original *historical context*. God spoke to his people through the events, words, manifestations and diverse manners and times spoken of in the Word of God. As believers in the power of the Holy Spirit to continue to use that Word in our lives, we explore what the text *meant* in its *historical context* in order to gain insight into what the text *means* to us today. Our intent in the *Three-Step Model* is to make neither historical nor grammatical blunders which would cause us to misinterpret the meaning of the text in its original context, so as to misapply its meaning in our own context today.

Finally, we affirm the Bible as a book of literature, and as such, must be studied in the context of its *genres within their own literary contexts*. Because the Bible is actually a library of texts of diverse literary material, some knowledge of the way in which particular types of literature work is extremely helpful in discerning the meaning of the message *through the literary genre and within the literary context*. The *Three-Step Model* takes into account the immediate context of the passage in connection to those paragraphs preceding and following it. We will also look at the passage in terms of its broader, more remote context, its place within a section of a chapter or book, and we will strive to make sense of the meaning of a text in light of its place in the entire work.

Even after these critical contextual issues are thoroughly assessed, we will encourage the students to become handy at the kinds of rules and principles associated with the different types of materials in Scripture. Are there specific rules of a poem that, once understood, may help us better understand the poetic works of the Scriptures? Are there issues underlying parables or stories which can help us master the biblical parables and better interpret the biblical stories? Using insights in this way may help us grasp the meaning of the text in a greater fashion.

Please notice again in the objectives that these truths are clearly stated. As usual, your responsibility as Mentor is to emphasize these concepts throughout the lesson, especially during the discussions and interaction with the students. The more you can highlight the objectives throughout the class period, the better the chances are that they will understand and grasp the magnitude of these objectives.

2
page 100
Devotion

This devotion focuses on the kind of heart preparation necessary to take full advantage of a critical approach to the Word of God. The Scriptures are in fact a book of literature, but it is unlike any other book in that it can transform the soul of the student who approaches it in such a way as to make its study an *encounter with God through Jesus Christ in the power of the Holy Spirit*. The goal of Bible study is not to settle curiosities or to find fuel for debate and argument; the Word for Ezra was life-shaping and life-transforming power that would allow him to relate to God in such a way as to become his vessel and instrument.

Paul Karleen has spoken eloquently of this life transforming dimension of the Word of God which in fact must impact the personal preparation and readiness of any serious student of the Bible:

> One of the most serious errors students of the Bible can make is to think that their labors alone determine what they will gain from Scripture. The divine Author of the Book is its ultimate Interpreter. The believer can count on the truth of 1 Cor. 2.12: "Now we have received, not the spirit of the world, but the Spirit who is from God, that we might know the things freely given to us by God" (NASB). Those who know Jesus Christ as Savior have the same Holy Spirit within them to illumine Scripture. Being regenerated is the first requisite to making sense of the Bible.
>
> Further, since God speaks to us through his Word, we should regard every occasion of reading or studying that Word as an encounter with God himself. The more you expect God to open divine truth to you, the more you must be willing to lay your spiritual state bare before God as

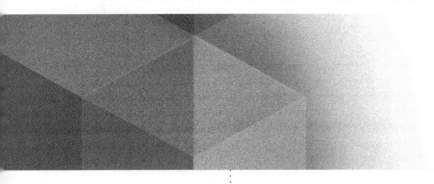

2

you open the Book. And the more clearly you understand it and the more you apply it to your life, the more spiritual needs it will reveal. It is the malleable heart that will glean the most from Scripture.

Although the Bible contains enough to challenge the greatest minds to lifelong study (and even they can never exhaust its content!), it is the personal appropriation and ultimate application of its truths which are at issue. Vance Havner understood this when he said:

> *The storehouse of God's Word was never meant for mere scrutiny, not even primarily for study but for sustenance. It is not simply a collection of fine proverbs and noble teachings for men to admire and quote as they might Shakespeare. It is ration for the soul, resources of and for the spirit, treasure for the inner man. Its goods exhibited upon every page are ours, and we have no business merely moving respectfully amongst them and coming away none the richer.*

> ~ Paul Karleen. *The Handbook to Bible Study.* (electronic ed.).
> New York: Oxford University Press, 1987.

Truly, the Bible is not meant to be merely scrutinized, as if you can read its message and then calmly walk away from it. Rather, in order for biblical interpretation to transform us we must see it as brother Havner suggested: as "ration for our souls, resources of and for the spirit, treasure for the inner man."

Challenge your students to adopt the kind of serious, sober, and passionate vision toward the Word that Ezra possessed, and perhaps the Holy Spirit will be so gracious as to grant us the same kind of impact he had on the people of God, for the glory of the Lord.

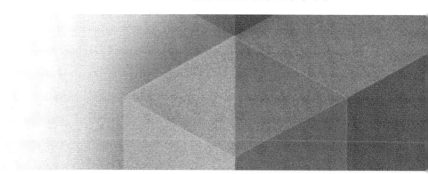

📖 **3**
page 118
Student Questions
and Response

Explore the definition, purpose, elements, and benefits of the *Three-Step Model* through the questions below. Your focus here ought to be helping your students master the critical claims and understandings associated with the model. Also, make the focus on the discussion their analysis of the material in light of the lesson aims presented at the beginning of the lesson. Of course, pay attention to your time issues, and concentrate upon those questions below and those posed by your students which get at the core of the material. Make certain, too, that you watch for any tangents which may lead you from rehearsing the critical facts and main points associated with understanding the rationale of the *Three-Step Model* of biblical interpretation.

📖 **4**
page 126
Counseling and Prayer

Challenge the students to apply the Word of God in community, in their company together as learners, as leaders, and as friends. The power of corporate prayer to touch the heart of the Lord and move his hand to work is well documented throughout Scripture, and is therefore a critical element in the application of the Word to our lives. Never give the impression during this section that you do this through formality and familiarity alone. Rather, encourage the students to fervently and wholeheartedly make their requests known to God, and to expect him to work as they, two or three together, are gathered in his name to pray (Matt. 18.20).

2

BIBLICAL STUDIES

The Old Testament Witness to Christ and His Kingdom
The Promise Given

📖 1
page 129
Lesson Introduction

Welcome to the Mentor's Guide for Lesson 3, *The Old Testament Witness to Christ and His Kingdom: The Promise Given.* The overall focus of this lesson is to help your students see how thoroughly and convincingly the OT communicates about Messiah as revealed in the person of Jesus Christ. It will be the thesis of this lesson that the OT's theme is the presentation of Christ, providing a window into the character, work, and glory of the coming Messiah, and it does this in a variety of ways and modes. In a real sense the OT foreshadows and anticipates the coming one, revealing him in the history of Israel, in analogical relationships with OT characters in its institutions and events, and in its moral righteousness and Messianic prophecies about the Redeemer and Anointed one to come. Fundamentally, this lesson is about hermeneutics, that is, how we are to read and interpret the Old Testament in a way that corresponds to its own internal coherence and structure.

For many students of the Bible, urban and suburban, we find today a general neglect and illiteracy of the OT text. And little wonder, it is a collection of remarkably diverse literature, oriented around an ancient people and culture, and communicates oftentimes in figurative and symbolic language. It is largely centered around the developing history of the people of Israel, and God's relationship with this people as the nation from which his own Messiah would come as the Savior and Redeemer of the world. What will be argued in this lesson is that the subject proper of the OT is its relationship to the Messiah revealed in Jesus Christ in the NT. This impulse to provide a sense of anticipation of the Messiah in the OT makes it intimately connected with the corresponding impulse in the NT, which is the revelation of the Messiah in Jesus of Nazareth.

The Old Testament's relationship to the New is specifically Christocentric: the OT offers the foundation of the hope and promise of the Messiah which is revealed and clarified in the NT. In this sense, we cannot understand the OT *on its own; uninterpreted by its appeal and application to the New Testament.* In terms of the history of Israel, the highlight of religious celebration and ceremony, its high moral teaching, and its predictions about the coming Messiah, the OT provides the groundwork for comprehending and appreciating the ministry of Jesus. This essential

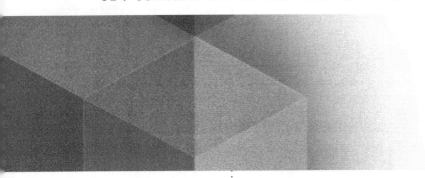

unity and continuity between the OT and the NT is the operating and guiding principle of this course. We will use the NT to make sense of the OT, and use the OT to clarify and illumine the message of the NT. Continuity and unity underlie the relationship between the testaments.

Norman Geisler, who arguably has written some of the most compelling arguments by any biblical scholar on the unity and continuity between the testaments, makes this relationship between the Old and New clear. He answers well the question, "What is the correct way to interpret the Bible?":

> What is the correct way to interpret the Bible? It is sometimes imagined that there are as many different interpretations of the Bible as there are readers. How should the Bible be understood? As the Ethiopian eunuch asked, with the Bible in hand, "How can I [understand] unless someone guides me?" The answer to this problem for the Christian is clear. Christ is our guide; he is the key to the interpretation of the Bible. Jesus claimed five times that he is the theme of the entire canon of Old Testament Scripture. Speaking of the Law and Prophets he said, "I have come not to abolish them but to fulfill them" (Matt. 5.17). Jesus walked with two disciples on the road to Emmaus, and "beginning with Moses and all the prophets, he interpreted to them in all the Scriptures the things concerning himself" (Luke 24.27). Later, to the ten disciples in the upper room Jesus said, "Everything written about me in the Law of Moses and the Prophets and the Psalms must be fulfilled" (Luke 24.44). In dialogue with the Jews Jesus charged, "You search the Scriptures . . . and it is they that bear witness to me" (John 5.39). The writer of Hebrews ascribes to Christ these words of Psalm 40: "It is written of me in the roll of the book" (Heb. 10.7). These five times our Lord affirmed that he is the theme of the whole Old Testament. We may conclude then, on the authority of Christ, that he is the theme of the entire Bible. The Bible must be interpreted Christocentrically (i.e., Christ centered). There is no other way for a Christian to understand it. There are at least three basic senses in which we may see Christ in the Bible as we survey its content: (1) Christ is the theme of both testaments of the Bible, (2) Christ is the theme of each of the eight sections of Scripture, and (3) Christocentric themes and truths may be found in each of the sixty-six books of the Bible. Like

a puzzle, once the overall picture (theme) is understood, it is much easier to put all the pieces together.

~ Norman L. Geisler. *A Popular Survey of the Old Testament.*
Grand Rapids: Baker Book House, 2003. p. 19-20.

Geisler nicely summarizes what will be the underlying theme of this lesson. We are hoping that your students will not be intimidated by the OT, but will see that with a Christocentric focus, they can master the theme of the OT. Understanding its structure in a Christ-centered and Christ-oriented way, they can gain a handle of its most fundamental message, and come to comprehend its inner structure in a way that usual methods of OT study cannot.

Throughout this lesson, then, you will want to encourage your students in their ability to gain a hold of the essential structure and data making up the very voluminous and remarkably diverse literature we call the Old Testament. This focus on a *Christo-centric hermeneutic* is the way that non-experts in the languages and culture of the OT can truly gain real intimate knowledge of the book's internal logic and operating principle. Just saying this, however, will not be convincing unless your students have an opportunity to see just how thoroughgoing the principle is in the literature. This lesson has been designed to show just how intimate the relationship between the material of the OT is with the person and work of Jesus Christ. This focus on the unity of the Scriptures, and, because of it, our ability to gain a real handle of its overall meaning and usage, are the critical themes of the lesson. Emphasize them as often as you can, and use the examples of a Christo-centric hermeneutic which are offered here as evidence of them both.

Notice at the beginning of each lesson that the teaching aims and objectives are prominently displayed. These aims represent the heart of the material and impulse behind all of the lecture and discussion of the lesson. We have sought to make them clear and direct. You ought to emphasize them throughout the lesson, during the discussions and interaction with the students. The more you can highlight the objectives throughout the class period, the better the chances are that they will understand and grasp the magnitude of these objectives.

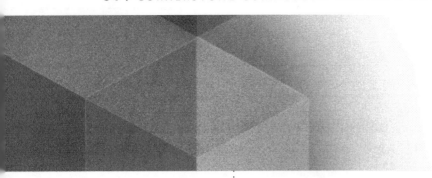

📖 **2**
page 129
Lesson Objectives

Again, the objectives represent the "residual message" (i.e., those ideas that, after all is said and done, we want the students to be left with) of the lesson. You ought to spend ample time reviewing them before the class session, and lead the entire learning event with a discussion of what they are, and why they are important. Do not hesitate to discuss these objectives briefly before you enter into the class period. Draw the students attention to the objectives, for, in a real sense, this is the heart of your educational aim for the class period in this lesson. Everything discussed and done ought to point back to these objectives. Find ways to highlight these at every turn, to reinforce them and reiterate them as you go.

📖 **3**
page 130
Devotion

This devotion focuses on the promise of God as the foundation and heart of both the structure and life of the OT, and its fulfillment in the NT. The most credible, simple, and compelling way to structure our understanding of the biblical materials is in the motif of *promise and fulfillment*: God from the beginning declared that he would send a Savior who would once and for all time remedy the situation that occurred due to the voluntary and senseless rebellion of our forbears, Adam and Eve, and the futile revolution of Satan against the authority and rule of God. This promise and its fulfillment represents the very structure of biblical revelation, and makes clear the relationship between the Old Testament (as expression of the promise), and the
New Testament (as its clarification and fulfillment).

Our English word "promise" is related to the Latin term *promissa*, defined in the Oxford Dictionary as "a declaration or assurance made to another person with respect to the future stating that one will do or refrain from some specified thing, usually in a good sense implying something to the advantage or pleasure of the person concerned". While the Hebrew does not appear to have a word that communicates specifically this meaning in particular, the idea of promise is clearly present in the use of *dabar*, translated hundreds of times in the way we use it today, i.e., promises made between people, or those made by Yahweh with his people (Deut. 1.11; 6.3; 9.28; 15.6; 19.8, 1 Kings 5.12, etc.).

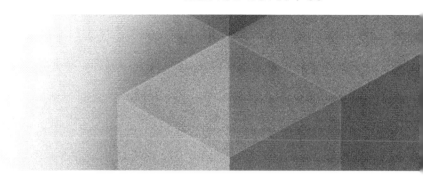

It may help you in your conversation with the students to understand better the nature of promise in the biblical record. For instance, the word *angelia* is the word for "promise" in the NT. In the vast majority of the cases it is translated simply as "promise," both as a noun and when used in its verbal form. Interestingly, the word *angelia* means "something that is announced." One of its cognate words *angelos* (from which we get our word "angel", is the one who announces or brings the message. The NT term for Gospel *euangelia* refers to a message or announcement of good news and good tidings. In a few instances it is used regarding promises made between people (cf. Acts 23.21).

Even a quick scan of the OT biblical materials reveals from the earliest texts the significance of promise in them, especially in regard to God's promise to provide an heir to Abraham (see Rom. 4.13-16, 20; 9.8-9; 15.8; Gal. 3.16-22; 4.23; Heb. 6.13-17; 7.6; 11.9, 11, 17). These promises provide the structure and shape of the entire history and experience of Abraham, his heirs (i.e., his descendants Isaac and Jacob), and the people which would spring from them and carry the hope of the seed of Abraham who would come bringing redemption and restoration to the people and the Land.

W. M. Smith highlights the importance of the concept of promise in a discussion of God's prophetic prediction that he would send an heir in promise to Abraham and a seed to sit on the throne of David, a "Savior according to promise" (Acts 13.23):

> Stephen speaks of the time of the advent as that in which "the time of the promise drew nigh" (Acts 7.17). This promise to David of a Savior has been confirmed in Christ (Acts 13.32). It is to this group that we must assign Paul's allusion to "the promise by faith in Jesus Christ" (Gal. 3.22). It is probable that this dual grouping of promises, those to Abraham concerning a seed and those to David concerning a king to reign, are united in Paul's references to this subject as "the promises made unto the fathers" (Rom. 15.8); in the familiar discussion of Israel's future, he refers to the Israelites as "the children of the promise" (Rom. 9.8-9) and reminds them that they are the ones who possess the promises of God (Rom. 9.4). Closely associated with this is the gift of God promised to us in Christ, that is, the promise of life in Christ (2 Tim. 1.1), or, as elsewhere

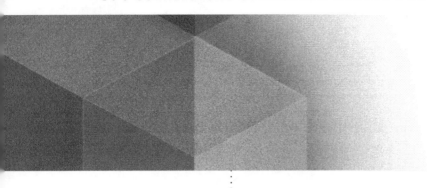

expressed, "the promise of eternal inheritance" (Heb. 9.15), or as John wrote, "the promise which he promised us, even the life eternal" (1 John 2.29).

~ W. M. Smith. "Promise." *The Evangelical Dictionary of Theology.* Walter A. Elwell, ed. (electronic ed.) Ellis Enterprises, Inc. Grand Rapids: Baker Book House, 1984.

The heart and soul of our salvation is rooted in the fidelity of God to keep his promises to his world, to humankind, to his friend Abraham, and through him, to all those who come to believe in Jesus of Nazareth as the Messiah and Lord, the fulfillment of the divine promise. In a real sense, the God and Father of our Lord Jesus Christ is the *original* Promise Keeper, the one who swore by himself to draw out of the world a people for his own possession. The writer to the Hebrews says that this knowledge of God's fidelity to his promise is an anchor to our souls, the very ground of our being:

> Heb. 6.17-19 – So when God desired to show more convincingly to the heirs of the promise the unchangeable character of his purpose, he guaranteed it with an oath, [18] so that by two unchangeable things, in which it is impossible for God to lie, we who have fled for refuge might have strong encouragement to hold fast to the hope set before us. [19] We have this as a sure and steadfast anchor of the soul, a hope that enters into the inner place behind the curtain.

Remind your students that the structure of the testaments aligns perfectly with the character of the living God whose promise and its fulfillment is the ground and confidence of our hope of eternal life, and the certainty of our ministries in the name of Jesus.

📖 **4**

page 134
Contact

The *Contact* section of the lessons is designed in order to aid you to "prime the pumps" of your students before you engage the lecture material, and your discussion after it. These are designed to give you an opportunity to introduce the students to the theme about to be considered, and to do so usually from a practical, interesting, and/

3

BIBLICAL STUDIES

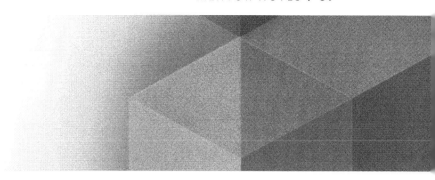

or controversial way. They are discussion starters, meant to focus the attention of the students on the material about to be studied. As such, they are the springboard into the material, not the proverbial pool. In other words, use them to arrest the students' attention and get them concentrated on the subject of the day. Be careful, however, that you do not take most of your actual lesson time on them. They are meant to introduce the lesson, not take the place of them.

📖 **5**
page 143
Student Questions
and Response

Discussing the material with the students is a critical element in the learning activity of each lesson. The following questions are designed to help you review the major concepts and claims brought out in the video. What you should aim to do is to engage the students in the ideas covered, making certain that you know that they have grasped the key ideas and the connections between them.

As you dialogue with your students, do not hesitate to explain the concepts as you go. Undoubtedly from time to time, they will encounter an idea or theme that both intrigues and/or confuses them. On these, as well as all of your dialogue time, you will have to gauge your time well, especially if your students are intrigued with the concepts, and want to discuss their implications at length.

📖 **6**
page 144
Summary of
Key Concepts

Listed below are the fundamental truths written in sentence form which the students should have received from this lesson, that is, from the video and your guided discussion with them. Make sure that these concepts are clearly defined and carefully considered, for their quiz work and exams will be taken from these items directly.

📖 **7**
page 146
Student Application
and Implications

The purpose of this section is to aid your students in applying the messages and truths of the Bible to their own individual lives. It is all too easy for us to dialogue and discuss the insights we have discovered in our investigation of the text and then miss its meaning for our

BIBLICAL STUDIES

3

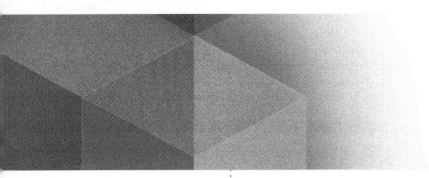

own lives. This section in every lesson is the opportunity for us to deliberately relate the truths to *our own lives and walk with the Lord.*

In helping your students think through their own situations, you might want to design some questions to help them apply the truths to their own lives. Feel free to use all or some of the questions provided below as a means to get the conversation going, to jump start the exploration into possible applications of the text. What is significant here is not the questions written below, but for you, in conversation with your students, to settle on a cadre of issues, concerns, questions, and ideas that flow directly from their experience, and relate to their lives and ministries. Do not hesitate to spend the majority of time on some question that arose from the viewing of the lecture, or some special concern that is especially relevant in their ministry context right now. The goal of this section is for you to enable them to think critically and theologically in regard to their own lives and ministry contexts.

Again, the questions below are provided as guides and primers, and ought not to be seen as absolute necessities. Pick and choose among them, or come up with your own. The key is relevance now, to their context and to their questions.

📖 **8**
page 147
Case Studies

The *Case Studies* are designed to force the students to engage in creative application of the truth to either a real or imagined situation, one which requires them to take seriously the relationship of the truth to real experience. The key is not that they discover the one "right answer" or "correct solution" to the situation, but learn how to carefully gather all of the facts, think through them carefully, and make application based on the what they have learned. These case studies, even the ones designed from the imagination, run closely with the kinds of issues and situations that urban leaders are likely to encounter, so encourage them to *think as leaders* as they engage in the discussions. This is not *pretension*, but *practice*, and, as the adage wrongly suggests, practice does not make perfect. Rather, *right practice* makes more *perfect.*

3

B I B L I C A L   S T U D I E S

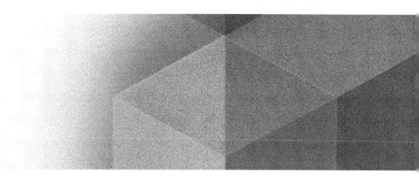

📖 **9**
page 150
Ministry Connections

The *Ministry Connections* section parallels the *Student Application and Implications* section in that it looks for direct and specific application to the student's context and situation. The main difference, however, is that the Ministry Connections section is concerned about their ability to think of how these truths relate to their *ministry practice and execution.* In other words, the intent is to help the students wrestle with the implications of the truths covered in the lesson in light of the ways in which they are currently caring for souls, teaching and preaching, or in any manner of their service to the Lord. This habit of constantly finding ways to apply the Word of truth to their lives is central in their *mature use of the Bible.* Note this principle as stated in the New Testament:

Heb. 5.11-14 – About this we have much to say, and it is hard to explain, since you have become dull of hearing. [12] For though by this time you ought to be teachers, you need someone to teach you again the basic principles of the oracles of God. You need milk, not solid food, [13] for everyone who lives on milk is unskilled in the word of righteousness, since he is a child. [14] But solid food is for the mature, for those who have their powers of discernment trained by constant practice to distinguish good from evil.

James 1.22-25 – But be doers of the word, and not hearers only, deceiving yourselves. [23] For if anyone is a hearer of the word and not a doer, he is like a man who looks intently at his natural face in a mirror. [24] For he looks at himself and goes away and at once forgets what he was like. [25] But the one who looks into the perfect law, the law of liberty, and perseveres, being no hearer who forgets but a doer who acts, he will be blessed in his doing.

Matt. 7.24-25 – Everyone then who hears these words of mine and does them will be like a wise man who built his house on the rock. [25] And the rain fell, and the floods came, and the winds blew and beat on that house, but it did not fall, because it had been founded on the rock.

Matt. 12.50 – For whoever does the will of my Father in heaven is my brother and sister and mother.

Matt. 28.20 – . . . teaching them to observe all that I have commanded you. And behold, I am with you always, to the end of the age.

3

BIBLICAL STUDIES

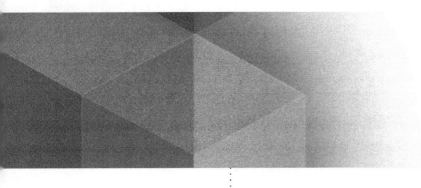

Luke 6.46-48 – Why do you call me "Lord, Lord," and not do what I tell you? [47] Everyone who comes to me and hears my words and does them, I will show you what he is like: [48] he is like a man building a house, who dug deep and laid the foundation on the rock. And when a flood arose, the stream broke against that house and could not shake it, because it had been well built.

Luke 11.28 – But he said, "Blessed rather are those who hear the word of God and keep it!"

Remind your students constantly that the study of the word of God is to lead to the transformation of their lives and the renewal of their minds (Rom. 12.2), not merely the filling of their notebooks, and the completion of their assignments! Help them probe for sensitive areas in their lives that they may apply the Word, and to do so promptly and fully.

📖 **10**
page 151
Counseling and Prayer

Helping the students understand the role of prayer in biblical interpretation is the reason for this section. We ought never to sever the acquisition of the wisdom of the Lord from requesting it from him:

James 1.5-6 – If any of you lacks wisdom, let him ask God, who gives generously to all without reproach, and it will be given him. [6] But let him ask in faith, with no doubting, for the one who doubts is like a wave of the sea that is driven and tossed by the wind.

1 Kings 3.7-9 – And now, O Lord my God, you have made your servant king in place of David my father, although I am but a little child. I do not know how to go out or come in. [8] And your servant is in the midst of your people whom you have chosen, a great people, too many to be numbered or counted for multitude. [9] Give your servant therefore an understanding mind to govern your people, that I may discern between good and evil, for who is able to govern this your great people?"

Prov. 3.5-7 – Trust in the Lord with all your heart, and do not lean on your own understanding. [6] In all your ways acknowledge him, and he will make straight your paths. [7] Be not wise in your own eyes; fear the Lord, and turn away from evil.

These texts show the intimate relationship between praying to the Lord for wisdom, acknowledging him in all our ways, and receiving his truth and insight. Do not consider, therefore, the time you pray with your students an overly familiar or unnecessary thing. Always remind them of the role of prayer in authentic spiritual discovery, and challenge them to share their questions with the Holy Spirit connected to the ideas and truths presented in the lesson. Prayer is a wonderfully practical and helpful way to apply truth; by taking specific needs to God in light of a truth, the students can solidify those ideas in their soul, and receive back from the Lord the answers they need in order to be sustained in the midst of their ministries.

Of course, everything is somehow dependent on the amount of time you have in your session, and how you have organized it. Still, prayer is a forceful and potent part of any spiritual encounter and teaching, and if you can, it should always have its place, even if it is a short summary prayer of what God has taught us, and a determination to live out its implications as the Holy Spirit teaches us.

📖 **11**
page 151
Assignments

A major part of your work with the students is ensuring that they are prepared for the *next class session* and all the various elements that they will need to be responsible for. They will need to review the material for the quiz, memorize the Scripture references for the class session, read their portion in the assigned text, and report their findings in a written short summary.

As to the written piece, remind them of what the particular goal is. In these lessons, the textbooks provide supplementary insights and complimentary truths to the outline material covered in the lessons. Their reading and writing assignment is not meant to either be difficult or discouraging. The ought to read the material as best as they can, and then write a few sentences on what they take them to mean. This is a critical intellectual skill for your students to learn, so make sure that you encourage them in this process.

Of course, for those students who might find this difficult, assure them of the intent behind this assignment, and emphasize their understanding

BIBLICAL STUDIES

3

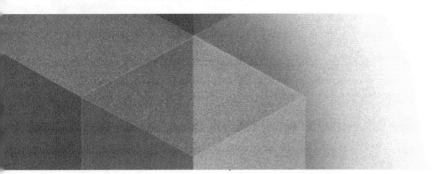

of the material being the key, not their writing skills. We want to improve their skills, but not at the expense of their encouragement and edification. Nor, however, do we want to sell them short. Strike to find the midpoint between challenge and encouragement here.

LESSON
4

The New Testament Witness to Christ and His Kingdom
The Messiah Opposed

📖 1
page 153
Lesson Introduction

Welcome to the Mentor's Guide for Lesson 4, *The Messiah Opposed*. The overall focus of this lesson is to highlight and detail the kind of social and spiritual opposition that Jesus faced as he fleshed out his Messianic ministry in Israel. What is critical for the students to comprehend is the intrinsic nature of conflict to the ministry of Jesus. This focus on the warrior nature of Jesus' ministry should be a key theme emphasized throughout this lesson. The fact that Jesus came to engage the powers is clear in the Scriptures, and should be the notable emphasis in your overall guidance of the class. The texts below can be helpful to you in leading your students in discussing the nature of the spiritual conflict that Jesus encountered.

Social Conflict

Isa. 53.3 – He was despised and rejected by men; a man of sorrows, and acquainted with grief; and as one from whom men hide their faces he was despised, and we esteemed him not.

Matt. 5.11 – Blessed are you when others revile you and persecute you and utter all kinds of evil against you falsely on my account.

Matt. 10.34-36 – Do not think that I have come to bring peace to the earth. I have not come to bring peace, but a sword. [35] For I have come to set a man against his father, and a daughter against her mother, and a daughter-in-law against her mother-in-law. [36] And a person's enemies will be those of his own household.

Matt. 10.21 – Brother will deliver brother over to death, and the father his child, and children will rise against parents and have them put to death.

Matt. 24.10 – And then many will fall away and betray one another and hate one another.

Mark 13.12 – And brother will deliver brother over to death, and the father his child, and children will rise against parents and have them put to death.

4

BIBLICAL STUDIES

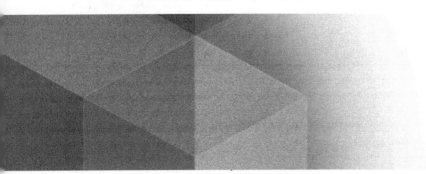

Luke 21.16 – You will be delivered up even by parents and brothers and relatives and friends, and some of you they will put to death.

Matt. 10.22 – and you will be hated by all for my name's sake. But the one who endures to the end will be saved.

Matt. 24.9 – Then they will deliver you up to tribulation and put you to death, and you will be hated by all nations for my name's sake.

Mark 13.13 – And you will be hated by all for my name's sake. But the one who endures to the end will be saved.

Luke 6.22 – Blessed are you when people hate you and when they exclude you and revile you and spurn your name as evil, on account of the Son of Man!

John 3.20 – For everyone who does wicked things hates the light and does not come to the light, lest his deeds should be exposed.

John 7.7 – The world cannot hate you, but it hates me because I testify about it that its works are evil.

John 15.18-25 – If the world hates you, know that it has hated me before it hated you. [19] If you were of the world, the world would love you as its own; but because you are not of the world, but I chose you out of the world, therefore the world hates you. [20] Remember the word that I said to you: "A servant is not greater than his master." If they persecuted me, they will also persecute you. If they kept my word, they will also keep yours. [21] But all these things they will do to you on account of my name, because they do not know him who sent me. [22] If I had not come and spoken to them, they would not have been guilty of sin, but now they have no excuse for their sin.

[23] Whoever hates me hates my Father also. [24] If I had not done among them the works that no one else did, they would not be guilty of sin, but now they have seen and hated both me and my Father. [25] But the word that is written in their Law must be fulfilled: "They hated me without a cause."

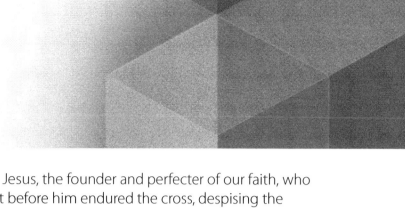

Heb. 12.2 – looking to Jesus, the founder and perfecter of our faith, who for the joy that was set before him endured the cross, despising the shame, and is seated at the right hand of the throne of God.

James 4.4 – You adulterous people! Do you not know that friendship with the world is enmity with God? Therefore whoever wishes to be a friend of the world makes himself an enemy of God.

1 John 3.1 – See what kind of love the Father has given to us, that we should be called children of God; and so we are. The reason why the world does not know us is that it did not know him.

1 John 3.13 – Do not be surprised, brothers, that the world hates you.

Spiritual Conflict

1 John 3.8 – Whoever makes a practice of sinning is of the devil, for the devil has been sinning from the beginning. The reason the Son of God appeared was to destroy the works of the devil.

Gen. 3.15 – I will put enmity between you and the woman, and between your offspring and her offspring; he shall bruise your head, and you shall bruise his heel.

Isa. 27.1 – In that day the Lord with his hard and great and strong sword will punish Leviathan the fleeing serpent, Leviathan the twisting serpent, and he will slay the dragon that is in the sea.

Mark 1.24 – "What have you to do with us, Jesus of Nazareth? Have you come to destroy us? I know who you are – the Holy One of God."

Luke 10.18 – And he said to them, "I saw Satan fall like lightning from heaven."

John 12.31 – Now is the judgment of this world; now will the ruler of this world be cast out.

John 16.11 – concerning judgment, because the ruler of this world is judged.

4

BIBLICAL STUDIES

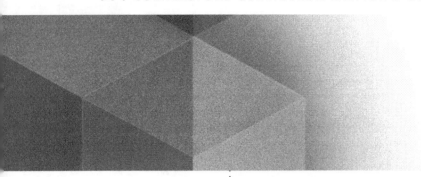

4

Rom. 16.20 – The God of peace will soon crush Satan under your feet. The grace of our Lord Jesus Christ be with you.

Col. 2.15 – He disarmed the rulers and authorities and put them to open shame, by triumphing over them in him.

Heb. 2.14 – Since therefore the children share in flesh and blood, he himself likewise partook of the same things, that through death he might destroy the one who has the power of death, that is, the devil.

1 John 3.5 – You know that he appeared to take away sins, and in him there is no sin.

Rev. 20.2-3 – And he seized the dragon, that ancient serpent, who is the devil and Satan, and bound him for a thousand years, [3] and threw him into the pit, and shut it and sealed it over him, so that he might not deceive the nations any longer, until the thousand years were ended. After that he must be released for a little while.

Rev. 20.10 – and the devil who had deceived them was thrown into the lake of fire and sulfur where the beast and the false prophet were, and they will be tormented day and night forever and ever.

📖 **2**
page 153
Lesson Objectives

Please notice again in the objectives that these truths are clearly stated. As usual, your responsibility as Mentor is to emphasize these concepts throughout the lesson, especially during the discussions and interaction with the students. The more you can highlight the objectives throughout the class period, the better the chances are that they will understand and grasp the magnitude of these objectives.

📖 **3**
page 153
Devotion

In order to understand the nature of conflict, a disciple must embrace this as a part of their normal, spiritual journey. Because our Lord suffered at the hands of those who neither knew God nor him, and because we are united to Christ by faith (Rom. 6.1-6), no believer or Christian leader need be shocked at persecution, as though something is happening to them that was unexpected or unplanned. This devotion focuses on

the inevitability of persecution on the lives of those who follow in the footsteps of Jesus. And the testimony of the Word of God bears this out:

1 Pet. 4.12-14 – Beloved, do not be surprised at the fiery trial when it comes upon you to test you, as though something strange were happening to you. [13] But rejoice insofar as you share Christ's sufferings, that you may also rejoice and be glad when his glory is revealed. [14] If you are insulted for the name of Christ, you are blessed, because the Spirit of glory and of God rests upon you.

1 Cor. 10.13 – No temptation has overtaken you that is not common to man. God is faithful, and he will not let you be tempted beyond your ability, but with the temptation he will also provide the way of escape, that you may be able to endure it.

1 Thess. 3.2-4 – and we sent Timothy, our brother and God's coworker in the gospel of Christ, to establish and exhort you in your faith, [3] that no one be moved by these afflictions. For you yourselves know that we are destined for this. [4] For when we were with you, we kept telling you beforehand that we were to suffer affliction, just as it has come to pass, and just as you know.

1 Pet. 5.9 – Resist him, firm in your faith, knowing that the same kinds of suffering are being experienced by your brotherhood throughout the world.

Acts 14.22 – strengthening the souls of the disciples, encouraging them to continue in the faith, and saying that through many tribulations we must enter the kingdom of God.

Rom. 8.35-37 – Who shall separate us from the love of Christ? Shall tribulation, or distress, or persecution, or famine, or nakedness, or danger, or sword? [36] As it is written, "For your sake we are being killed all the day long; we are regarded as sheep to be slaughtered." [37] No, in all these things we are more than conquerors through him who loved us.

1 Cor. 4.9 – For I think that God has exhibited us apostles as last of all, like men sentenced to death, because we have become a spectacle to the world, to angels, and to men.

4

BIBLICAL STUDIES

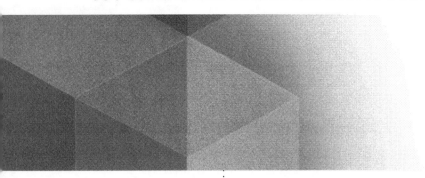

4

BIBLICAL STUDIES

2 Tim. 3.11-12 – my persecutions and sufferings that happened to me at Antioch, at Iconium, and at Lystra – which persecutions I endured; yet from them all the Lord rescued me. [12] Indeed, all who desire to live a godly life in Christ Jesus will be persecuted.

1 Pet. 2.21 – For to this you have been called, because Christ also suffered for you, leaving you an example, so that you might follow in his steps.

Highlight this significant spiritual truth as you discuss with the students their reaction to the devotional.

📖 **4**
page 154
Contact

It should not surprise you if you get a great variation of responses and opinion from your students concerning the inevitability of suffering and opposition in the Christian life. Depending upon the spiritual diet they are accustomed to, students may respond, on the one hand, to this as a no-brainer, a clearly articulated truth that lies at the very center of the Word of God's testimony about any who affiliate with the Messiah. On the other hand, if the diet of the students tend toward "health-wealth" cuisine, then such teaching will not be seen as helpful. It may even be seen as mildly dismissive of the victory won for us by Christ, and at worst even heretical. Regardless of the initial reaction, it is important to make certain that the students understand the central role that this teaching plays in Jesus' teaching, as well as the clear model he provides in his own life. The opposition that believers must endure is intrinsic to their allegiance to Messiah. All those who hate him will instantly hate them as well, and they must be prepared for this onslaught and rejection from those who do not know him.

📖 **5**
page 155
Summary

Here again it is critical to track carefully not merely the social conflict which Jesus encountered with his contemporaries in Israel, but perhaps most importantly to track his constant and ongoing battle with the spiritual forces which sought to undermine his ministry. Satan and his minions play a dramatic role in the Gospel drama, and no full

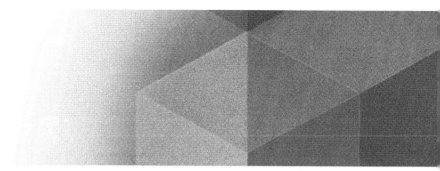

understanding of the life and ministry of Jesus is possible that underestimates or overlooks these critical dimensions.

The Nature of Demons in Scripture

In order to understand Jesus' ongoing conflict with the powers of evil in this age, you should introduce to the students briefly and carefully the subject of demons. I say briefly and carefully because we are not exhorted in the New Testament to become experts on the ways of the "dark side." Rather, we are told not to become ignorant of his schemes (e.g., 2 Cor. 2.11 – "so that we would not be outwitted by Satan; *for we are not ignorant of his designs*"), and to be alert to his machinations at all times because of his desire to devour anyone he can (e.g., 1 Pet. 5.8-9 – "Be sober-minded; be watchful. Your adversary the devil prowls around like a roaring lion, seeking someone to devour. [9] Resist him, firm in your faith, knowing that the same kinds of suffering are being experienced by your brotherhood throughout the world").

Although the Old Testament does not seek to speculate much on the subject of dark spirituality, it is clear that some links are connected with the work of the enemy and the practices of idolatry, magic, and witchcraft forces (Deut. 32.17; Ps. 96.5). These practices were against the Law and will of God, they were strictly forbidden to God's community (Deut. 18.10-14; 1 Sam. 15.23). As one scholar suggests, demonic activity in the Old Testament is largely to be understood as an "opposing force to God and his own personal intermediary beings, the *malakim* (angels)."

In the New Testament, the terms associated with these spirits are *daimon* and *daimonion*, the actual presence of these beings is defined as "unclean" (*akatharton*, Mark 1.24-27; 5.2-3; 7.26; 9.25; Acts 5.16; 8.7; Rev. 16.13) and "evil" (*ponera*, Acts 19.12-16) spirits. The majority of texts in reference to the activity of these spirits connect them to the possession of individuals. While the New Testament does not seek to give a systematic answer as to where these beings originated, there is no question that they exist in the mind of the New Testament writers, and that they operate against the affairs of Christ and his work.

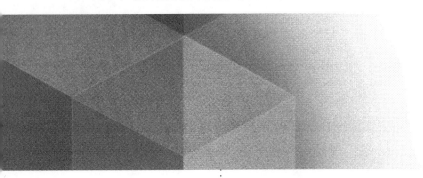

There is a strong connection to the activity associated with these beings and idolatry (cf. Paul's understanding of the link to idols and demons in 1 Corinthians 10.20-21; 12.2; cf. Rev. 9.20). Paul and John indicate that demonic activity will increase as the end draws near, with very powerful effects of deception and seduction of others (1 Tim. 4.1; Rev. 16.13-14). Christians are to be engaged with these powers, even as our Lord was, as detailed in Ephesians 6.10-18. The Christian must be prepared to combat "rulers . . . authorities . . . powers, this dark world and the spiritual forces of evil in the heavenly realms."

What is crucial to emphasize here is that the coming of Messiah was directly related to overcoming the forces of evil, including those effects of the curse and powers of evil which sought to interfere with God's reassertion of his rule over his creation.

📖 **6**
page 168
Case Studies

These case studies are designed to evoke open dialogues and conversations about some of the implications associated with modern views of suffering, opposition, conflict, and triumph in the Christian life. What is important to note here is that these issues are some of the most common and pervasive in the Church, especially in the American church which tends to think of the Christ victory in terms of health, wealth, and blessing. This view of the Christian life is so common that many take it to be the only credible reading and interpretation of the meaning of Christ's life and death for us today. To revisit this question is critical, especially for those planting churches and making disciples in neighborhoods amidst populations which are poor, disenfranchised, broke, and dangerous. Encourage your students to wrestle with these concepts, for they lie at the base of an entire cadre of related issues that arise from the different frameworks of Christian spirituality which believers adhere to today.

📖 **7**
page 171
Counseling and Prayer

In this lesson, which highlights the issues of suffering, opposition, and conflict, it should be plain that an emphasis on prayer is appropriate. If you can, seek to spend a good amount of time in this lesson on prayer, especially since this was Jesus' surest and most common way to receive

from the Father the grace, instruction, and leading he needed in order to endure the constant onslaught of his worldly foes and invisible enemies. In this, we ought to model the example of Christ and the Apostles, who made prayer a significant ongoing discipline in their lives.

> Luke 6.12-13 – In these days he went out to the mountain to pray, and all night he continued in prayer to God. [13] And when day came, he called his disciples and chose from them twelve, whom he named Apostles.

> Matt. 14.23-25 – And after he had dismissed the crowds, he went up on the mountain by himself to pray. When evening came, he was there alone, [24] but the boat by this time was a long way from the land, beaten by the waves, for the wind was against them. [25] And in the fourth watch of the night he came to them, walking on the sea.

> Mark 6.46 – And after he had taken leave of them, he went up on the mountain to pray.

> Col. 4.2 – Continue steadfastly in prayer, being watchful in it with thanksgiving.

Also, do not consider it an overly familiar or unnecessary thing to ask the students if they need prayer for someone or something connected to the ideas and truths presented in the lesson. Prayer is a wonderfully practical and helpful way to apply truth; by taking specific needs to God in light of a truth, the students can solidify those ideas in their soul, and receive back from the Lord the answers they need in order to be sustained in the midst of their ministries. Of course, everything is somehow dependent on the amount of time you have in your session, and how you have organized it. Still, prayer is a forceful and potent part of any spiritual encounter and teaching, and if you can, it should always have its place, even if it is a short summary prayer of what God has taught us, and a determination to live out its implications as the Holy Spirit teaches us.

4

BIBLICAL STUDIES

Theology and Ethics

LESSON
1

The Kingdom of God
God's Reign Inaugurated

📖 **1**
page 179
Lesson Introduction

Welcome to the Mentor's Guide for Lesson 1, *The Kingdom of God: God's Reign Inaugurated.* The goal of this lesson is to provide your students with a biblical framework to understand what God is doing in human history, and prepare them to be able witnesses of Christ and his Kingdom. This lesson is designed to show the students how God's reign has been infiltrating the world since the time of the Fall; God has not abandoned his creation, but has covenanted to bring to himself a people who would be his forever, through the salvific work of his Son, Jesus Christ. Adopting the mindset and disposition of a warrior, God covenanted with Abraham to bless all the families of the earth through his line, and thus, God determined to restore his reign to the earth. God renewed the covenant through the patriarchs, his people Israel, through the tribe of Judah and the family of David. Finally, in the fullness of time, Jesus of Nazareth appeared, whose presence represents the realization of the Kingdom on earth. Through his death, burial, resurrection, and ascension, the rule of God has come in power. While the consummation of the Kingdom is still future, at the Second Coming of Christ, the Kingdom of God has come in the person of Jesus. This high theology represents the teaching aims of this lesson, *God's Reign Inaugurated.*

Please notice again in the objectives that these truths are clearly stated. As usual, your responsibility as Mentor is to emphasize these concepts throughout the lesson, especially during the discussions and interaction with the students. The more you can highlight the objectives throughout the class period, the better the chances are that they will understand and grasp the magnitude of these objectives.

📖 **2**
page 179
Devotion

The theme of today's lesson is the inauguration of the Kingdom of God, not in terms of a single event, but in the sense of an unfolding vision, with the presence of Jesus Christ representing the culmination of the Kingdom's announcement. In a real sense, God began the announcement of his rule restored to earth with the *proto-evangelium*, the first telling of the Good News in Genesis 3.15. In the announcement that the serpent's head would be crushed by the Seed of the woman, God announced his resolve to bring order and beauty back to the earth, which was marred through the rebellion and disobedience of humankind and the great

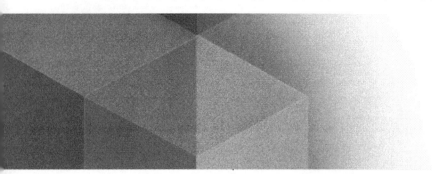

THEOLOGY AND ETHICS

prince, the devil. This quiet, confident announcement of the Kingdom of God being "at hand" or "near" suggests that with Jesus' presence in the world, the Kingdom has come.

📖 **3**
page 180
Contact

The contacts of this lesson all deal with identifying the beginning and/or start of God's resolve to restore the Kingdom of God to earth. The notion of beginning is key, not only for introducing the Lesson, but will also be critical for the application of the truths in this session. For instance, knowing that God's initiative lies at the heart of all of his salvific work is critical for our own attitude of thanks to God, as well as the confidence that we hold that the work of the Kingdom is in fact God's own work. God is the worker, and we are coworkers with him in his harvest, for "we are God's fellow workers. You are God's field, God's building" (1 Cor. 3.9, ESV). God is the primary actor in the drama of salvation, and our role is to participate with God as co-workers in his vineyard. The heart of this contact is emphasizing the issues of the students, of course, but to do so in light of this central truth.

📖 **4**
page 181
Summary

This lesson focuses on the realization of the Kingdom's presence in the person of Jesus of Nazareth. In a real sense, Jesus is the King whose person is the ground of his authority. In other words, who Jesus is becomes the basis of his Sovereign Majesty and authority. Jesus of Nazareth performs in his life and ministry the role of Yahweh's King, calling a people out of the world that would be his peculiar possession (Isa. 55.5; John 10.16, 27). As Lord and King, Jesus has provided to his people his own judgments and standards which ought to regulate the operations and actions of his people in every way they govern themselves (1 Cor. 5.4-5; 12.28; Eph. 4.11-12; Matt. 28.19-20; 18.17-18; 1 Tim. 5.20; Titus 3.10). It is his kingly power and authority by which he protects, supports, and preserves his people in the midst of their tribulations, conflicts, and trials for his name's sake (2 Cor. 12.9-10; Rom. 8.35-39), and through his kingly authority received from his Father, he as Lord

defeats, constricts, and marshals his power to limit the influence and effects of his enemies (Acts 12.17; 18.9-10; 1 Cor. 15.25). As the one appointed by God to have all authority in heaven and on earth, he commands and arranges all things to exist for his greater glory and honor, and determines the inherent good in all things (Rom. 8.28; 14.11; Col. 1.18; Matt. 28.19-20). And as Judge, he will one day execute the righteous sentence of the Father upon all those who reject the good news of the Kingdom, and will himself take vengeance on those refusing his reign and disobeying his Gospel (Ps. 2.9; 2 Thess. 1.8).

📖 **5**
page 182
Outline Point I

Jesus' entrance into the world represents a new level of intensity and focus to the Lord's divine battle to restore his reign in the world. In a real sense, Jesus of Nazareth intensifies the battle of the Kingdom in the world by focusing not so much on human sin and evil, but on the malevolent powers of the Evil One, and the spiritual powers and principalities. Jesus inaugurates the Kingdom with genuine violence against the kingdom of the devil, but he does not fight the battle with spear and sword, but with the weapons of spiritual warfare in the Holy Spirit. For instance, when Peter resorts to the use of the sword in protection of Jesus, he rebukes him and goes to the cross instead, which is the ultimate secret weapon of the Kingdom of God (Matt. 26.50-56).

This notion of Jesus as the supreme Warrior and Christ's death on the cross as the ultimate weapon is described by Paul in Colossians where he speaks of Jesus' death as disarming the powers and authorities (Col. 2.15), and their ultimate defeat through the cross. Jesus' death and ascension are figured as a classic kind of victory celebration, a parade of the great General who brings the spoils and prisoners of war in his mighty Victor's train. This notion can be seen also in Ephesians 4.7-8, with its quotation from Psalm 68, a classic hymn of divine warfare. Amazingly, our Lord Jesus defeated the foes of God and inaugurated the Kingdom, winning the greatest battle of all on the cross, by being killed, not by physically killing others.

THEOLOGY AND ETHICS

1

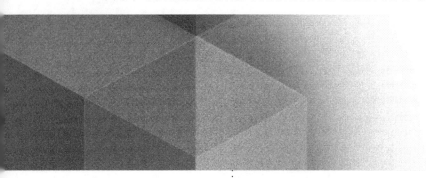

In a sense Jesus establishes in his coming the prototype and standard of all legitimate spiritual warfare. We defeat the enemy not by destroying others' lives, but by sacrificing our lives for them; we win the battle against the enemies of God not by killing human beings, but by living as living sacrifices, acceptable to God (Rom. 12.2; John 12.25). We win not by the power of the gun, the knife, and the missile, but by the Word of God and the shield of faith (Eph. 6.10-18). Jesus' defeat of the enemy proves that a significant portion of the fight deals with our own internal struggles against evil remaining within (Rom. 7.7-25; 2 Cor. 10.1-6).

6
page 183
Outline Point I-D

This idea, that in the coming of Jesus Christ the Kingdom was made visible in the world, is a significant revelation in the fulfillment of God's covenantal promise to restore his reign in the earth. With Jesus we experience the coming of the Messianic age in reality, not merely as an idea or hope or longing, but in actual fact.

G. E. Ladd makes this point explicitly when he suggests:

> Jesus proclaimed that this Promise [the Promise of the coming of the Kingdom] was actually being fulfilled. This is no apocalyptic Kingdom but a present salvation. Jesus did not promise his hearers a better future or assure that they would soon enter the Kingdom. Rather he boldly announced that the Kingdom (Herrschaft) of God had come to them. The presence of the Kingdom was "a happening, an event, the gracious action of God." The promise was fulfilled in the action of Jesus: in his proclamation of good news to the poor, release to the captives, restoring sight to the blind, freeing those who were oppressed. This was no new theology or new idea or new promise; it was a new event in history. "The wretched hear the good news, the prison doors are open, the oppressed breathe the air of freedom, blind pilgrims see the light, the day of salvation is here."

~ G. E. Ladd. *The Presence of the Future.*
Grand Rapids: Eerdmans Publishing, 1974. pp. 111-112.

📖 **7**
page 189
Conclusion

In light of all that Jesus of Nazareth accomplished through his death, resurrection, and ascension, his work as Divine Warrior in ushering in the Kingdom of God is not yet completed. A simple reading of the book of Revelation and the other apocalyptic portions of the New Testament reveal that he will fulfill the ministry that he inaugurated in his life, death, resurrection and ascension. Jesus himself spoke of the mighty day when he as the Son of Man would come on the clouds of heaven with the holy angels, to defeat finally and exhaustively all the powers that would resist his will (Mark 13.26). This vision and language mirrors the great vision of the prophet Daniel, who refers to a similar personage in Daniel 7.13. The Kingdom of God comes with violence, just as John the Baptist predicted it would come. Our Lord, who came the first time to execute God's secret weapon of the cross on his enemies, will in fact return again, this time as the true Divine Warrior whose work is public, exhaustive, and devastating for his enemies. Revelation 19.11-16 describes the coming of our Lord Jesus Christ in classic Divine Warrior imagery; he comes on a white horse, draped with a cape dipped in blood, with a two-edged sword coming from his mouth. Behind him are the veritable armies of heaven as he "judges and makes war" (v. 11).

The final vision of the Bible regarding Jesus as God's Divine Warrior wraps up the revelation with a remarkable picture of the last battle, which, at the very least, must be a rich and potent symbol of the final judgment to come, and of the vengeance and wrath God dispenses on those who have resisted his rule without repentance. In a real sense, Jesus of Nazareth is the Anointed One, the one chosen by God to end the conflict which began with the rebellion of the serpent and the disobedience of the first human pair. It is he who will crush to pieces the one *kakos*, the one who through his lies and deceptions inflicted misery and suffering upon the earth (Rom. 16.20; Rev. 12.9), and who represents the worst form of stubborn resistance to the rule of God. The promise of Genesis 3.15 has now finally come to pass in the person of the gentle Nazarene, who does the warfare of God, not by killing but by dying and rising again on behalf of those he came to save.

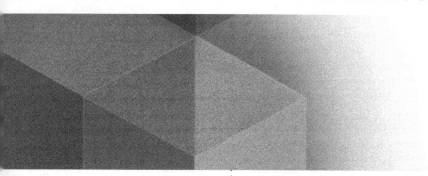

8
page 190
Student Questions
and Response

The goal of these segue questions is not that you feel the need to go through each one of them. Not only would this be laborious and tiresome, it might also deflect you from focusing on many of the tough issues and central concerns of your students. While the segue questions are meant to help you ensure that the students understand the concepts covered in the video, you will have to balance that objective with the obvious goal of dealing with their questions and interests as they respond to the Scriptures and other materials.

9
page 192
Case Studies

One of the goals in covering the case studies in this lesson is making specific and critical interconnections with what is arguably very difficult eschatology and the practical outworking of ministry in the city. One of the most challenging things for students to do is to see the correlation between the scriptural teachings on the Kingdom and their own lives and ministries. Whether or not you use the case studies below or choose to invent your own scenarios to discuss, you must seek to make the intersection plain between what the students have heard, learned, and discussed, and what they are confronted with in their ministries. In light of this, the case studies below try to take seriously what would occur if there might be inappropriate or exaggerated emphases on the Kingdom as already present, or if it were conceived as being entirely future. Believe it or not, the way in which an urban minister views this theology will have a profound impact on how they approach ministry and proceed in their own work for the Lord.

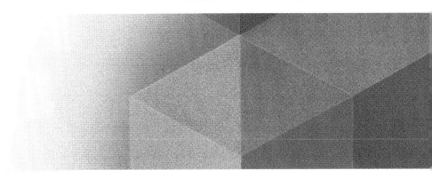

📖 **10**

page 194
Counseling and Prayer

Do not consider it an overly familiar or unnecessary thing to ask the students if they need prayer for someone or something connected to the ideas and truths presented in the lesson. Prayer is a wonderfully practical and helpful way to apply truth; by taking specific needs to God in light of a truth, the students can solidify those ideas in their soul, and receive back from the Lord the answers they need in order to be sustained in the midst of their ministries. Of course, everything is somehow dependent on the amount of time you have in your session, and how you have organized it. Still, prayer is a forceful and potent part of any spiritual encounter and teaching, and if you can, it should always have its place, even if it is a short summary prayer of what God has taught us, and a determination to live out its implications as the Holy Spirit teaches us.

1

THEOLOGY AND ETHICS

God the Father
The Triune God – The Greatness of God

 1

page 197
Lesson Introduction

Welcome to the Mentor's Guide for Lesson 2, *God the Father: The Triune God – The Greatness of God.* We will introduce to the students the idea of the Trinity, the biblical concept relating to the triune nature of God as Father, Son, and Holy Spirit. This cannot possibly be covered fully in the time frame allotted to us by the video teaching. What is possible, however, is that we provide a skeleton outline of the major issues associated with both of these interrelated doctrines which will allow the students to continue their study of these important subjects in the months and years to come.

As you lead your students to engage the teaching of the Trinity, seek to keep in mind four simple ideas that can guide you as you discuss this important doctrine with them.

First, *remember that God is one God.* There are not two Gods in the Bible, one in the Old Testament and the other in the New Testament. The same God is in both testaments, and the nature of God receives a fuller and more comprehensive display in the New Testament through Jesus Christ, who provides a complete and comprehensive knowledge of the Father to us (cf. John 1.14-18).

Second, God *reveals himself to us in three distinct personalities all involved in the salvation event, and yet God remains one undivided unity.* As you will see as you explore the texts in this lesson, that the Father reveals himself in the Son and Spirit without in any way ever melding personality with them, or they as persons with the Father's person. The Godhead is diverse yet unified.

Third, *we can grasp the Trinity best as we understand the role of each person in the plan of salvation.* The Father purposes, the Son executes, and the Spirit applies the blessing of redemption in the believer and in the Church. The New Testament doesn't speculate about the essence of the Godhead, but rather reveals what each person does in regards to the salvation won for us through Christ.

Fourth, *the scriptural doctrine of the Trinity cannot be plumbed by an appeal to logic and analysis alone; it remains for us an absolute mystery.* While there have been numerous attempts to make plain the meaning of the biblical teaching of the Trinity, it simply ought not surprise us that

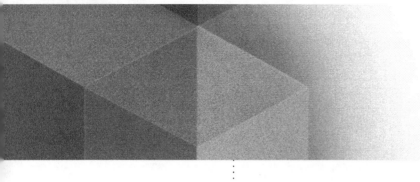

no human explanation can fully comprehend the glory and splendor of the nature of the persons of the Godhead, Father, Son, and Holy Spirit. As you and your students explore the Word of God in this lesson, I trust that you will allow both your humility and your diligence to express themselves in this study. Undoubtedly, both will be needed!

📖 2
page 197
Devotion

This devotion focuses on the *absolute mystery* in seeking to comprehend the Lord as a tri-unity.

Although the term *trinity* is not found in the Bible, it has become the term coined to make plain the teaching of Scripture of God's unity subsisting in three distinct Persons. This term comes from the Greek word trias, and was first used by Theophilus (A.D. 168-183). Another use came from the Christian apologist and advocate Tertullian (A.D. 220), who was the first to use the Latin term trinitas to lay out this doctrine.

While in the immediate post-biblical era believers in the Church sought to explain the doctrine of God's tri-unity in terms and language that was compelling and coherent philosophically, the use of various Greek ideas helped only some to make sense of God's nature. It appears that the Church has tended to shift from the plain confessions of the New Testament on how the Father, Son, and Holy Spirit act in salvation to more abstract discussions about the precise nature of the Godhead's very inner working. While such efforts are valiant, they cannot possibly provide final understandings of the Trinity.

I believe that there is another way, a simpler way. We can appeal to mystery and faith. The Trinity as a doctrine is not the result of trying to use Greek ideas to explain the God of Abraham. Rather, it comes from wrestling with the meaning of the Old and New Testament Scriptures which speak of a God who manifests himself in three persons, Father, Son, and Holy Spirit, and yet does not in any way assert himself as three gods, or as one God who takes three different forms for various purposes. This great God of Scripture reveals himself in Christ, who by the Holy Spirit fulfilled the purposes of his Father for the sake of saving the world.

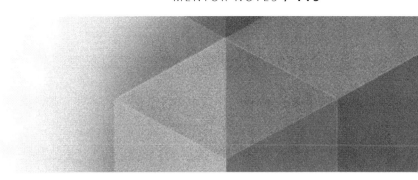

David's testimony in the little Psalm 131 is a veritable gold mine of insight for us as we seek to delve into the depths of the Lord's own person:

> Ps. 131.1-3 – O Lord, my heart is not lifted up; my eyes are not raised too high; I do not occupy myself with things too great and too marvelous for me. [2] But I have calmed and quieted my soul, like a weaned child with its mother; like a weaned child is my soul within me. [3] O Israel, hope in the Lord from this time forth and forevermore.

Let us then assert the plain language of the Bible: God is one.

> Deut. 6.4 – Hear, O Israel: The Lord our God, the Lord is one.

> 1 Kings 8.60 – . . . that all the peoples of the earth may know that the Lord is God; there is no other.

> Isa. 44.6 – Thus says the Lord, the King of Israel and his Redeemer, the Lord of hosts: "I am the first and I am the last; besides me there is no god."

But let us also assert that Jesus is the Word made flesh (John 1.14), and affirm the Holy Spirit as Lord and life-giver to the Church (2 Cor. 3.17-18).

Let's allow the authors of our textbooks to have the last word here:

> The Church has not hesitated to teach the doctrine of the Trinity. Without pretending to understand, she has given her witness, she has repeated what the Holy Scriptures teach. Some deny that the Scriptures teach the Trinity of the Godhead on the ground that the whole idea of trinity in unity is a contradiction in terms; but since we cannot understand the fall of a leaf by the roadside or the hatching of a robin's egg in the nest yonder, why should the Trinity be a problem to us? "We think more loftily of God," says Michael de Molinos, "by knowing that he is incomprehensible, and above our understanding, than by conceiving him under any image, and creature beauty, according to our rude understanding."
>
> ~ A. W. Tozer. *The Knowledge of the Holy.*
> New York. Harper San Francisco, 1961. p. 18-19.

"Glory be to the Father," sings the Church, "and to the Son, and to the Holy Ghost." What is this? we ask – praise to three gods? No; praise to one

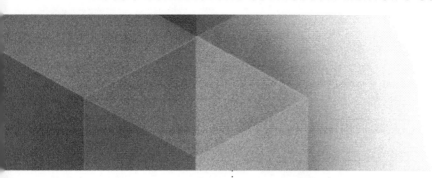

God in three persons. As the hymn puts it, "Jehovah! Father, Spirit, Son! Mysterious Godhead! Three in One!" This is the God whom Christians worship – the triune Jehovah. The heart of Christian faith in God is the revealed mystery of the Trinity. Trinitas is a Latin word meaning threeness. Christianity rests on the doctrine of the trinitas, the threeness, the tripersonality, of God.

~ J. I. Packer. *Knowing God.*
Downers Grove: InterVarsity Press, 1993. p. 65.

📖 **3**
page 199
Contact

In a time where formal teaching of God's revelation concerning himself is considered "theological baggage," it is important to remind the students of what is at stake in right belief about God. Both of their texts affirm the importance of seeing and understanding God aright, in sync with what he has revealed himself to be to us. Our responsibility is to discover God as he is, and not as we think him to be, and want him to be.

That our idea of God correspond as nearly as possible to the true being of God is of immense importance to us. Compared with our actual thoughts about him, our creedal statements are of little consequence. Our real idea of God may lie buried under the rubbish of conventional religious notions and may require an intelligent and vigorous search before it is finally unearthed and exposed for what it is. Only after an ordeal of painful self-absorbing are we likely to discover what we actually believe about God.

~ A. W. Tozer. *The Knowledge of the Holy.*
New York: Harper San Francisco, 1961. p.2.

One can know a great deal about God without much knowledge of him. I am sure that many of us have never really grasped this. We find in ourselves a deep interest in theology (which is, of course, a most fascinating and intriguing subject – in the seventeenth century it was every gentleman's hobby). We read books of theological exposition and apologetics. We dip into Christian history, and study the Christian creed. We learn to find our way around in the Scriptures. Others appreciate our interest in these things, and we find ourselves asked to give our

opinion in public on this or that question, to lead study groups, to give papers, to write articles, and generally to accept responsibility, informal if not formal, for acting as teachers and arbiters of orthodoxy in our own Christian circle. Our friends tell us how much they value our contribution, and this spurs us to further explorations of God's truth, so that we may be equal to the demands made upon us. All very fine – yet interest in theology, and knowledge about God, and the capacity to think clearly and talk well on Christian themes, is not at all the same thing as knowing him. We may know as much about God as Calvin knew – indeed, if we study his works diligently, sooner or later we shall – and yet all the time (unlike Calvin, may I say) we hardly know God at all.

~ J. I. Packer. *Knowing God.*
Downers Grove: InterVarsity Press, 1993. p. 26.

Remind the students that what is at stake in trinitarian study is quite literally *our very knowledge of God as he has revealed himself to us.* It means that everything is at stake in studying God as he is.

📖 **4**
page 211
Student Questions
and Response

Tozer's claims regarding the trinity are as true today as the first moment he thought and penned the following words:

> The doctrine of the Trinity is truth for the heart. The spirit of man alone can enter through the veil and penetrate into that Holy of Holies. "Let me seek Thee in longing," pleaded Anselm, "let me long for Thee in seeking; let me find Thee in love, and love Thee in finding." Love and faith are at home in the mystery of the Godhead. Let reason kneel in reverence outside.

~ A. W. Tozer. *The Knowledge of the Holy.*
New York: Harper San Francisco, 1961. p. 20.

Your discussion of the truths regarding the Trinity should concentrate not on trying to solve the mystery of the Godhead, but understanding the "lay of the land" so to speak in biblical and theological studies concerning the Trinity. Focus on the major points of trinitarian doctrine: the unity of God, three persons sharing the same substance in the Godhead, the

distinctiveness of the members of the Trinity. By focusing on the main points you can set a framework in which we not only help the students to master this data, but will also give them a way to study this important subject in the future.

📖 **5**
page 214
Case Studies

These case studies seek to explore the significance of belief in God as Trinity for both life and ministry. Help the students consider what is at stake in someone denying the truth of the Scriptures regarding the person of God, and help them define the boundaries of what is considered acceptable in terms of different beliefs regarding the Trinity.

📖 **6**
page 217
Assignments

By the end of the second class session, you ought to have mentioned to the students the need for them to have given some thought and spadework to their Ministry Project. Now, by the end of the third lesson, you should also have emphasized their need to select a passage for their Exegetical Project. Both of these assignments tend to "creep up on" the students at the end of the course, so make sure that you emphasize with them the work to be done, the standards for doing it, and the dates when the work will be due. Give them proper notice on the final and any other assignments, and exhort them to be organized and ready for the work ahead.

Do not fail to emphasize these matters to your students for, as in all study, the end of the course is hectic, with many things becoming due and the students feeling the pressure to do many things at once to meet due dates. Any way that you can remind them of the need for advanced planning will be wonderfully helpful for them, whether they realize it immediately or not.

Because of this, we advocate that you consider docking a modest amount of points for late papers, exams, and projects. While the amount may be nominal, your enforcement of your rules will help them to learn to be efficient and on time as they continue in their studies.

God the Son
Jesus, the Messiah and Lord of All – He Died

📖 **1**
page 219
Lesson Introduction

Welcome to the Mentor's Guide for Lesson 3, *God the Son: Jesus, the Messiah and Lord of All – He Died.* The focus of this lesson is to try to help the students capture the data as well as the mystery that surrounds the passion, suffering, and death of our Lord. This need to be aware of the meaning of his death is central to all that this lesson will seek to reveal and make known.

What will be immediately obvious for you and your students is the diversity of opinions about the nature and meaning of Christ's death. What is critical here is to see that the various emphases, while containing elements of truth, must be overruled and understood in light of the teaching of the Scriptures themselves. This is not to be wooden and mean-spirited in our assessment of the various kinds of perspectives which have come to be associated with his passion and death. Rather, it is to say that our lesson will focus more on the plain, transparent meanings of Jesus' death given to us by the biblical texts themselves.

As you walk through the various views with the students, it will be important that you stay as close as possible to the New Testament's emphasis of Christ's death, especially with its focus salvifically on his substitutionary (also called vicarious, meaning "in the place of another") death on behalf of sinners. Texts such as Isaiah 53, 1 Timothy 2.6, and 1 Peter 2.24 emphasize this kind of vision of Christ's death as a *death for us*, on our behalf (see also 2 Corinthians 5.21; 1 Peter 3.18 emphasizing his death on behalf of all humanity).

Make certain that your own emphasis parallels that of the apostles, who tend to refuse a *monolithic* approach to the meaning of Jesus' death. For instance, Jesus' death provides redemption; we have been bought with a price, purchased out of the slave market of Satan and sin to live free as God's servants (2 Cor. 6.20 with 1 Cor. 7.23; Gal. 3.13; 4.5; Rev. 5.9; 14.3-4). Furthermore, we have been reconciled to God, restored out of the estrangement and alienation we had with him due to our own voluntary rebellion against his will (Rom. 5.10; 2 Cor. 5.18-21). His death also propitiated us before the Lord, satisfying all the claims of our holy God and making a way for his divine wrath to be satisfied and his compassion to be poured out even on guilty Gentiles (Rom. 3). Through his death we are forgiven of our sins (Col. 2.13) and our sins

are sins sent away from us through Christ's death for us (cf. Matt. 6.12; 9.6; James 5.15; 1 John 1.9). We are now declared righteous though his death, and have peace with God through faith in Jesus (Rom. 5.1).

With all of these and other rich images of the wealth attained for us through the death of Christ, it will be important for you to model the important trait of multiple right answers in regards to the death of the Son of God for us. Model in your discussion and manner the importance of taking a symphonic approach to the meaning of Christ's death. Many things have been accomplished by our Lord, and our goal should be to enable our students to recognize and celebrate this important truth.

As usual, pay close attention to the objectives in this lesson. They will help guide you into the kind of recognition of the riches of Christ that are associated with his passion and suffering on our behalf.

📖 **2**
page 219
Devotion

This devotion focuses on the vicarious nature of our Lord's death, which is so critical for an understanding of our participation in Christ's death, and our continued carrying of our cross before him. Christ did not die in a vacuum; his death was a direct punishment upon his divine person on account of the very acts that we have committed countless thousands of times. It was our rebellion, our disobedience, our foolishness, and our cruelty that caused him to endure the rejection and wrath of his Father in our place.

Often, it is possible to turn the death of Jesus into an abstract conversation about theological issues, obtuse notions about things that the human mind was never meant to know. Rather than embracing the plain and direct meaning of Scripture, we hide our true complicity in the torture and murder of Christ by eclipsing it with big words about "propitiation" and "justification." When, in fact, his hair was yanked out, he was punched in the face, and his back was cut to ribbons with the lash because of our own personal guiltiness before God. We have trampled God's law, and Jesus' painful death was his loving answer to it. Through the death of Jesus, my own personal sin is redeemed.

This kind of reflection immediately reveals the real purpose of Christological understanding: the worship and love of our great God and Father, through Jesus Christ. God's unsought, eternal, remarkable love was demonstrated through the cruel beatings, scourgings, humiliations, and ultimately the horrific death of our Lord on the cross. The wonder of God's love ought not merely produce shiny essays on bright white paper, but broken souls, humbled before God and ready to be used in the same way that our dear Lord humbled himself and became obedient unto death, even death on the cross.

Seek to make the deep feeling and heart language plain here, and not only in the devotion, but throughout the entire lesson. Enable your students to see and sense the horrifying spectacle it was when our dear Lord put himself in our place to bear the inequity and rebellion that we have so heartlessly and foolishly manifested from childhood.

Truly, our Lord died because the Father laid on him the iniquity of us all.

📖 3
page 222
Contact

The contacts in this lesson are designed to help prime the pump of our understanding about both the *fact of* and the *meaning and implications of* the death of Christ. This is one of the most important and yet difficult tasks for us as leader developers. How and in what ways do we help emerging Christian leaders to rediscover the meaning of the death of Jesus, when in so many contexts that death has been underestimated, over-abstracted, and virtually ignored as the heart and soul of Christian faith and life, both in terms of its *objective* work, resulting in our salvation and redemption, and its *subjective* work, i.e., our duty to take up our cross and to follow him, *being conformed to his death*?

As you proceed through this lesson, be especially cognizant of the present-day tragedy of a kind of mind-less (over against mindful) comprehension of the death of Jesus. Our aim must be to help reintroduce this momentous truth with both clarity and freshness, in order that our students can discover before them the Lord displayed as crucified before them. Paul suggests this is possible in his critique of the Galatian malady to ignore the far-reaching implications of the death of Christ for salvation and for discipleship. (Gal. 3.1 – O foolish Galatians!

3

THEOLOGY AND ETHICS

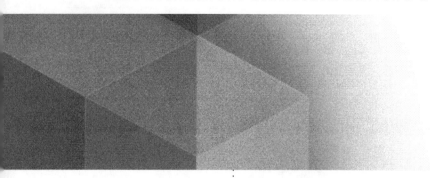

Who has bewitched you? It was before your eyes that Jesus Christ was publicly portrayed as crucified.)

📖 **4**

page 234
Student Questions
and Response

The questions below seek to cover the critical claims associated with Christ and his death. The NT exposition of the meaning and method of Christ's death on the cross includes a wonderful variety of important images which you must help your students both understand and discuss during this section of the lesson. A number of places interweaves and explains these models, including texts such as 2 Corinthians 5.14-6.2 and Romans 3.24-26. Romans 6.1-11 speaks even of our own participation in his death, the killing of our flesh, and our sharing in the resurrection expressed in the living of a new life.

What you should seek to do in this discussion is to ensure that the students understand the main outline of the key NT images about the nature of Christ's death, and the primary benefits that this cursory summary made.

📖 **5**

page 235
Student Application
and Implications

What you must help your students understand in this section is the *richness of the imagery* associated with the work and the benefits of Christ's work on the cross. The tendency for young theologians to be reductive (boiling everything down to a single point) and *uncharitable* (failing to respect and listen to those with opposing viewpoints) is one which we must constantly be on guard against. We ought rather to strive to enable them to be *open-minded* (ready to see more than one side of an issue) and able to *suspend judgment* (until all positions have been heard and understood).

L. L. Morris provides us with a nice summary of the richness of the biblical view of Christ's atoning work in Scripture.

> Christ's atoning work is viewed from a number of angles. Thus sinners are slaves to their sin (John 8.34), but Christ has set them free (Gal. 5.1). They were caught up in the sin of Adam: 'in Adam all die' (1 Cor. 15.22). But Christ died for our sins (1 Cor. 15.3) and the effects of

Adam's sin have been nullified (Rom. 5.12-21). Sinners are subject to judgment, both a judgment in the here and now (Rom. 1.24, 26, 28) and a judgment at the end of the age (Rom. 2.16), but there is no condemnation for those who are in Christ (Rom. 8.1). We are captive to the law of sin (Rom. 7.23), while from another angle no-one will be justified by the works of the law (Rom. 3.20). But we are discharged from the law, dead to that which held us in bondage (Rom. 7.4). That the wrath of God is exercised towards sinners is in much modern theology an industriously evaded doctrine, but it is plain in the NT (Luke 3.7; John 3.36; Rom. 1.18; 2.5; etc.). But there is also the clear teaching that Christ has turned that wrath away from sinners (1 Thess. 1.10; 5.9). This is the meaning of propitiation too (Rom. 3.25; 1 John 2.2). Death is another tyrant (Rom. 6.23) from which Christ has freed us (Rom. 5.17; 1 Cor. 15.52-57). The flesh is evil (Gal. 5.19-21; Eph. 2.3), but it has been crucified in those who are Christ's (Gal. 5.24). There is a futility about much of life in this world, but Christians are delivered from it (Rom. 8.20-23); their lives are not in vain (1 Cor. 15.58; Phil. 2.16). The 'world' is hostile to Christ (John 7.7; 15.18), but he has overcome it (John 16.33). The plight of sinners is many-sided, but view it how you will, Christ has saved his people by his atoning death.

~ L. L. Morris. "Atonement." *New Dictionary of Theology.*
S. B. Ferguson, ed. (electronic ed.).
Downers Grove, IL: InterVarsity Press, 2000. p. 55.

Strive to help the students in this discussion to see the multi-sided and deeply textured biblical images of Christ's work on the cross, and seek to apply those meanings to their own particular and specific life situations.

📖 6
page 240
Assignments

By the end of the last class session, you ought to have emphasized your students' need to have done the necessary spadework to prepare for their Ministry Project. Also, certainly by this time in the unit, your students should have selected their biblical passage for their upcoming Exegetical Project. Both will be done with far better thought and excellence the earlier the students begin to think through them and decide what they want to do. Do not fail to emphasize this, for, as in all study, at the end of the course many things become due, and

THEOLOGY AND ETHICS

3

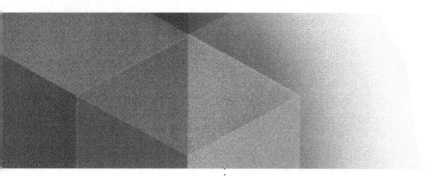

the students will begin to feel the pressure of getting a number of assignments in at the same time. Any way that you can remind them of the need for advanced planning will be wonderfully helpful for them, whether they realize it immediately or not.

Because of this, we advocate that you consider docking a modest amount of points for late papers, exams, and projects. This is not done to shame or harm the students, but to serve as a prod to get them in gear for their work, lest through procrastination they are forced to cram their assignments in at the last moment, sacrificing both excellence and thoughtfulness in the process on both of the projects. While the amount may be nominal, your enforcement of your rules will help them to learn to be efficient and on time as they continue in their studies.

LESSON
4

God the Holy Spirit
The Person of the Holy Spirit

📖 **1**
page 241
Lesson Introduction

Welcome to the Mentor's Guide for Lesson 4, *God the Holy Spirit: The Person of the Holy Spirit.* The overall focus of this lesson is to enable your students to understand who the Holy Spirit is (person) and what he does (work), to be able to defend this understanding from the Scriptures, and to see the implications of these truths for ministry in and through the Church.

The focus of this lesson is, first, to establish that the Holy Spirit is a Divine Person; second, to understand his relationship to the other members of the Holy Trinity; and third, to affirm that he is the Divine Life-giver who creates, sustains, and renews physical and spiritual life.

Notice in the objectives that these aims are clearly stated, and you ought to emphasize them throughout the lesson, during the discussions and interaction with the students. The more you can highlight the objectives throughout the class period, the better the chances are that they will understand and grasp the magnitude of these objectives.

📖 **2**
page 241
Lesson Objectives

Do not hesitate to discuss these objectives briefly before you enter into the class period. Draw the students attention to the objectives, for, in a real sense, this is the heart of your educational aim for the class period in this lesson. Everything discussed and done ought to point back to these objectives. Find ways to highlight these at every turn, to reinforce them and reiterate them as you go.

📖 **3**
page 241
Devotion

This devotion focuses on the fact that the person who wants to know God is dependent on the ministry of the Holy Spirit. As you begin this lesson on the Holy Spirit, it is undoubtedly true that you have some students who are *confident* about their ability to understand and complete the material and some who are *apprehensive*. Usually these attitudes come from past experiences with schooling. Students who have been successful at academics in the past tend to be confident while students who have struggled or failed tend to be apprehensive. This devotion gives you an opportunity to talk about those feelings. While learning theology does involve study, hard work, and thinking skills; it

4

THEOLOGY AND ETHICS

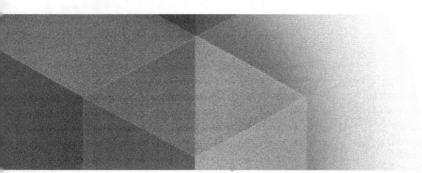

4

THEOLOGY AND ETHICS

is not completely the same as other academic disciplines. Our minds cannot comprehend God in his infinite mystery and unfathomable purposes. Being smart or academically experienced is no reason for confidence that a person will truly understand God. On the contrary, when we human beings come to the study of God, all of us stand on a level playing field: he is completely beyond us! Therefore, any true understanding of God will come through the gracious work of the Holy Spirit. Confident students should humbly acknowledge that their ability to memorize facts or manipulate concepts will not make them into theologians. They are completely dependent on the Spirit for true understanding. On the other hand, apprehensive students should be assured that if God has made them leaders in his Church and has brought them to this class for training, his Spirit is more than able to give them wisdom and understanding for the task. They, too, are completely dependent on the Spirit of God. Everyone who receives training in theology must come to rely on the promise of Christ:

> John 14.26 – But the Helper, the Holy Spirit, whom the Father will send in my name, he will teach you all things and bring to your remembrance all that I have said to you.

📖 **4**

page 242
Contact 1

As you introduce this assignment, please assure the students that you are not looking for high quality art work! Give the students 2-3 minutes to think of an idea and put it down on paper. After students have finished drawing, invite them to share their drawings with the whole group if the class is small, or break into small groups to share if the class is large. As each student shares they should explain why they chose to draw what they did and how it represents the Holy Spirit to them.

Transition to lesson: "People often have a difficult time understanding and relating to the Holy Spirit. Since it is common in our lives to be around fathers and sons, we have some starting point for understanding what it means to talk about God the Father or God the Son. It is much tougher to relate the title "Holy Spirit" to anything in our everyday experience. As we go through the lesson, stay alert for ideas that make it easier to understand who the Holy Spirit is and how we can explain this to others."

5
page 242
Contact 2

The doctrine of God is at the very root of everything else we believe about reality. If we have a wrong view of who God is, that misperception will ultimately distort everything else we believe. That is why the great heresies faced by the Church have almost always involved teaching something wrong about the nature of God. Help the students think of what would be lost to the Church if the Holy Spirit was only thought of as spiritual energy or spiritual consciousness (similar to "the force" portrayed in the Star Wars movies). For example, a spiritual force is not "holy," it cannot hate sin or love righteousness; a spiritual force cannot teach Jesus' disciples how to apply his words; a spiritual force cannot intercede for us in prayer; a spiritual force can bring God's power to us but not his personal loving presence, etc.

6
page 243
Contact 3

In answer to the first question: We mean that there is one God eternally existing in three persons: Father, Son, and Holy Spirit.

In answer to the second question, some illustrations might include:

Example 1: The Trinity is like water which can exist as solid (ice), liquid, or gas (steam). The strength of this illustration is that it shows how something common to our experience can appear in three different forms without changing its essential nature. The weaknesses would include that water is not all three forms at the same time and that water is an impersonal substance rather than a conscious being.

Example 2: The Trinity is like a man who is simultaneously a father, and husband, and a son. The strength of this illustration is that it involves a personal being and it builds upon the Father/Son language of the Trinity itself. The weakness is that it involves one person playing three roles. The man does not have three separate centers of consciousness; he is not three persons. Without proper explanation it could lead to thinking of the Trinity as Modalism does. Modalism is the heresy that denies the Trinity by teaching that God is a single person who, throughout biblical history, has revealed himself in three modes, or forms. According to Modalism, there are not three Persons in the Godhead, but one Person playing three different roles. (Note: Modalism is commonly refuted by appealing to Jesus' baptism where the Father speaks and the Spirit

4

THEOLOGY AND ETHICS

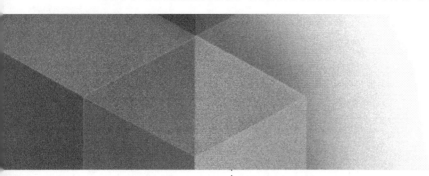

descends at the same time as Jesus is baptized or to the crucifixion where Jesus feels abandoned by the presence of the Father. In these and other instances we see the Father, Son, and Spirit relating to each other, something that they could not do if they were one person playing separate roles).

Have students think of and discuss a few of these illustrations and how they help us or hinder us in thinking rightly about God.

Transition: "Our lesson today will help us discover what the role of the Holy Spirit is in the life of the Trinity. We will try to find ways to describe the difference between the Son of God and the Spirit of God and we will try to discover the ways in which the Spirit relates to the Father and the Son. Some of these ideas will be difficult because we are talking about a great mystery but the Church has learned from experience how important it is to think rightly about the nature of God and to correct wrong ideas whenever they appear. No matter how difficult these theological ideas about the Trinity are, we should remember that the most basic truths of the Trinity can be learned by memorizing the Nicene Creed which describes the essential truths about God's nature in just a few paragraphs."

📖 **7**
page 244
Outline Point II-B-1

In Scripture it is not always obvious whether a verse refers to wind, to breath, to the human spirit, to an angelic or demonic spirit, or to the Spirit of God. That is why sometimes when you compare translations you will see one that translates a verse a breath and another as Spirit, or one capitalizes the word "Spirit" because it assumes the Spirit of God is being spoken of while another does not capitalize it because they assume that a person's spirit is under discussion.

Compare:

- Zech. 12.10 in the King James Version and New King James Version of the Scriptures. Compare "the spirit of grace and of supplications" and "the Spirit of grace and supplication."

- Ezekiel 37.9 in the English Standard Version (below), the New American Standard (NASB), and the New English Bible (NEB) versions of the Scriptures. Note the references to the Spirit: "breath," "spirit," and "wind."

Ezek. 37.9 (ESV) – Then he said to me, "Prophesy to the *breath*; prophesy, son of man, and say to the *breath*, Thus says the Lord God: Come from the four winds, O *breath*, and breathe on these slain, that they may live."

📖 **8**
page 245
Outline Point II-B-2

John Calvin follows the ancient theologians of the Church in distinguishing between the members of the Trinity in the following manner:

This distinction is, that to the Father is attributed the beginning of action, the fountain and source of all things; to the Son, wisdom and counsel, and arrangement in action, *while the energy and efficacy of action is assigned to the Spirit* [emphasis mine].

~ *Institutes*, I.xiii.18.

While all three persons are fundamentally united in every action take by God, we can speak of God the Father as being the basis of each action, God the Son (Logos) as ordering each action, and God the Spirit powerfully accomplishing each action. Thus the Old Testament view of the Spirit as the power of God in action is completely harmonious with the role of the Spirit found in the fully Trinitarian theology of the New Testament.

NOTE: When we talk about the functions of each person in the Trinity we are speaking about the "economic doctrine of the Trinity" (i.e. the ways in which Father, Son and Spirit act toward their creation) as opposed to the "ontological doctrine of the Trinity" (i.e. the ways in which the Father, Son and Spirit exist – i.e., the Father always begetting [generating], the Son always begotten, and the Spirit always proceeding).

4

THEOLOGY AND ETHICS

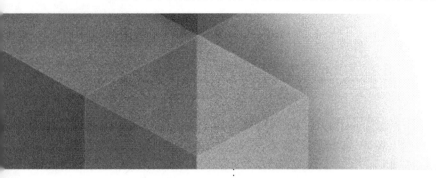

📖 **9**

page 249
Outline Point III-B-2-d

[T]he most striking appearance of dove imagery in the Bible belongs to the baptismal narratives where the Spirit of God descends from heaven "like a dove" (Matt. 3.16). . . . [O]ne should probably think of Genesis 1.2, where the Spirit of God, water, and the image of a bird recur (*merahepet* = "move" or "hover" is avian imagery, cf. Deuteronomy 32.11). The Talmud (b. Hag. 15a) likens the brooding of the Spirit over the waters at creation to the fluttering of a dove, and 4Q521, a Dead Sea Scroll fragment, gives Genesis 1.2 an eschatological reapplication: the Spirit will hover over the saints in the latter days. So the dove at baptism seemingly means that Jesus brings a new creation.

~ Leland Ryken, James C. Wilhoit and Tremper Longman III, Gen. ed.
"Dove." *Dictionary of Biblical Imagery.*
Downers Grove, IL/Leicester, England: InterVarsity Press, 1998. p. 217.

📖 **10**

page 251
Conclusion

Help the students to see that the entire ministry of the Holy Spirit has an ultimate goal and purpose. The goal of God is a new heavens and a new earth, inhabited by a new humanity (the Church), and united in perfect harmony under the rule of Christ. The Spirit is not just sustaining the present world but is actively working to accomplish God's ultimate purpose of a new creation.

📖 **11**

page 251
*Summary of
Key Concepts*

Listed below are the fundamental truths written in sentence form which the students should have received from this lesson, that is, from the videos and your guided discussion with them. Make sure that these concepts are clearly defined and carefully considered, for their quiz work and exams will be taken from these items directly.

📖 **12**

page 252
*Student Application
and Implications*

In helping your students think through their own situations, you might want to design some questions or use those provided below as water to "prime the pump" of their interests, so to speak. What is significant here is not the questions written below, but for you, in conversation with your students, to settle on a cadre of issues, concerns, questions, and

4

THEOLOGY AND ETHICS

ideas that flow directly from their experience, and relate to their lives and ministries. Do not hesitate to spend the majority of time on some question that arose from the video, or a special concern that is especially relevant in their ministry context right now. The goal of this section is for you to enable them to think critically and theologically in regards to their own lives and ministry contexts. Again, the questions below are provided as guides and primers, and ought not to be seen as absolute necessities. Pick and choose among them, or come up with your own. The key is relevance now, to their context and to their questions.

📖 **13**

page 253
Case Study 1

Responding to false teaching by Christian cults is where "the rubber meets the road" for Christian theological education. The goal of this case study is to check and see whether your students can defend the personality of the Holy Spirit from Scripture using their own words. This is important to practice because virtually every Christian leader will have to do this at some point in their ministry. As the students go through their responses, remind them that there are two things a pastoral leader must respond to. First, they must respond to the content of the quote, correcting and refuting the false teaching. But second, they must also respond to the person. What tone should be taken with Sue? Is she a "fierce wolf" (Acts 20.29; 2 John 10-11) deliberately trying to undermine the flock?; or, is she a misguided and confused seeker in need of pastoral teaching and care (2 Tim. 2.24-26)?

📖 **14**

page 254
Case Study 2

The key to this case study is for students to realize the power of Jesus' statement in John 14.16 that he is sending the Holy Spirit to be "another Helper [paraclete]." The Holy Spirit always faithful represents and acts in the place of Christ for us. Just as Jesus could claim that anyone who had seen him had seen the Father (John 14.9), it is equally true that anyone who has seen Jesus will recognize the Spirit that he sends. The Spirit's indwelling unites us to the living Christ so that we are joined to his love, his mind, his words, and his actions, as branches to a vine. We recognize Jesus and respond to him in faith through the illuminating work of the

THEOLOGY AND ETHICS

4

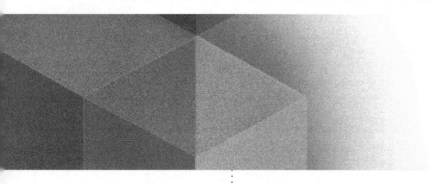

Holy Spirit and we recognize the Spirit and respond to him because he faithfully represents Christ and his teachings.

📖 **15**
page 255
Counseling and Prayer

In this opening session it is particularly important that you begin to build relationships with your students. Let them know that you care personally about them and their ministry calling. They are not just "students" but Christian leaders. They should see that you view this class, not primarily as an academic exercise, but as a way of equipping them to build up the Church and fulfill God's purposes. Encourage the class to share real situations they are facing in ministry this week and spend time praying for and encouraging each other.

📖 **16**
page 256
Assignments

Make certain that the students understand the assignment for next week, especially the written piece. This is not difficult; the goal is that they would read the material as best as they can and write a few sentences on what they take them to mean. This is a critical intellectual skill for your students to learn, so make sure that you encourage them in this process. Of course, for those students who might find this difficult, assure them of the intent behind this assignment, and emphasize their understanding of the material being the key, not their writing skills. We want to improve their skills, but not at the expense of their encouragement and edification. Nor, however, do we want to sell them short. Strike to find the midpoint between challenge and encouragement here.

4

THEOLOGY AND ETHICS

Part III

Ministry
& Mission

MINISTRY & MISSION
UNIT 1

Christian Ministry

Theology of the Church
The Church at Worship

📖 **1**

page 267
Lesson Introduction

Welcome to the Mentor's Guide for Lesson 1, *Theology of the Church: The Church at Worship*. The goal of this lesson is to help students understand the Church as a community of people who have experienced the grace of God and who respond to this grace by engaging in worship as their duty and their delight.

The lesson will focus on the fact that salvation is all by grace since this is the starting point for a response of worship. It will also talk about the Lord's Supper and baptism as two of the most significant ways that the Church acknowledges, experiences, and responds to the grace of God. Since there are legitimate differences about the nature of the Lord's Supper and baptism among evangelical believers, please be prepared for disagreements among your students about what the Bible teaches and be ready to lead a discussion that is fair-minded and which helps students to develop their own convictions in light of Scripture and their denominations' theology.

Since the focus of this lesson is on worship, be sure that you cultivate "warm hearts" as well as "clear minds" on these issues. Students should be led to active thanksgiving and praise during these lessons as well as reflection on the theological issues involved. Please read the following objectives carefully. The more you can highlight the objectives throughout the class period, the better the chances are that they will understand and grasp the essential truths that underlie this lesson.

📖 **2**

page 267
Devotion

This devotion focuses on the motive of all God-honoring praise and worship: the incomparable glory of the person of God, Father, Son, and Holy Spirit. Often we may think that worship involves a certain kind of ritual action, ceremonial process, or liturgical order. The worship of God is not rooted in geography or religious orthodoxy, but, as Jesus says, in "spirit and in truth" (John 4.24). The Father cannot be approached except in the person of Jesus Christ (John 14.6), whose atoning sacrifice has brought us near to God in faith (Heb. 10.22-24). Because God has granted us entrance into his presence, even the Holy of holies through the blood of Jesus, and because God's glory is unmatched and unchanging, there

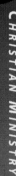

remains a ready reason to give glory and honor to God. We need never wait for circumstances to be warm and wonderful in order to praise God; even in the midst of the most horrible tragedy, the severest loss, the most disarming trouble, and the greatest need, we are to give praise and glory to God. In spite of all we face and know, he is the Lord of all, perfect, glorious, majestic, full of splendor and wonder, who will never forsake us or abandon us. Regardless of how things look, God is and remains forever by our side and for our benefit. Learning to give the "sacrifice" of praise, to change the meaning of the term for a moment, is a central skill of the developing disciple of Jesus. Countless times we will face situations where there does not appear, at least on the surface of the situation, a single reason to praise. All is wrong and bleak; God appears to have vanished, either not knowing, not caring, or being unable to help. In the midst of this kind of trouble, we grab our harps and give glory to the One who gives us life and sustains our days. He is worthy because he is, for his name is "I Am that I Am." Challenge the students to their truest vocation, the unbroken and unyielding praise of Almighty God because of who he is and what he has done in Jesus Christ.

📖 3
page 268
Scripture
Memorization
Review

The Psalmist affirms the power of the Word of God to keep our way pure (Ps. 119.9), to protect from the power of sin (Ps. 119.11), and to give life to the one who receives them (Ps. 119.93). Do not turn the Scripture memorization time into merely a class assignment drill, full of routine and boring repetition. Use this time to challenge and instruct the students on the benefit and profit of the memorized Word. Memorize the Scripture along with the students, and review with them where you are able. Discuss the Scripture's meaning, and how it relates thematically to what was covered in the lesson last week. This portion of the lesson may very well be the most important, so treat it with the requisite importance and respect. It is simply too easy to get overwhelmed and to treat the memorized Word as simply something to accomplish for the lesson's requirement. As mentor, attempt to safeguard this time from this deadly error.

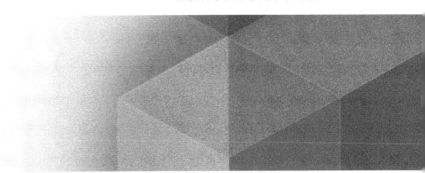

📖 **4**
page 269
Contact 1

Have students share briefly in groups how this realization occurred. (There is not time for everyone to give their entire testimony so make sure students hone in on the specific point of when they grasped that the could not earn salvation). Bring students back together and say "The Church exists only because of the grace of God. Today's lesson helps us understand worship as the Church's response to grace."

📖 **5**
page 269
Contacts 2 and 3

Both of these last two contact portions deal with a similar theme, that is, the character and quality of our worship, and what it is that God requires or demands. What is significant in considering worship here is the cultural and social norms associated with the practices and events deemed to be worship. In other words, churches are largely unaware that their worship is culturally and historically conditioned, and that worship of God, as an expression of truth and the heart, must have a deeply personal and immediate characteristic to it. It will never be worship simply to ape what others have done, expecting the feelings and affections that they had to be reproduced in us by the mere doing of their acts, the singing of their songs, or the practice of their deeds. Worship, as an expression of the Spirit, will always be dressed in cultural garments but it will also always be given to the God-above-all-cultures, the God and Father of our Lord Jesus. Gaining flexibility in worship styles and methods is directly correlated to seeing that God is a God of all humankind, and therefore can be legitimately and wonderfully glorified through the heartfelt cultural expression of any people who have repented, believed, and are following through faith, hope, and love the Son of God, Jesus Christ. Equating some cultural expression of worship with *worship itself*, that is, the way in which all worship everywhere is to be conceived and done, is a common and yet devastating error made in many congregations, and by many Christians. Allowing freedom to express our deepest gratitude and praise to God is a critical part of a leader's ministry in leading others into the presence of God.

1

CHRISTIAN MINISTRY

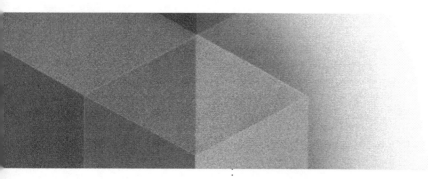

1

CHRISTIAN MINISTRY

📖 **6**
page 271
Outline Point I-C

Theologians often divide grace into descriptive categories. *Common grace* refers to God's providence over all people by which he sustains life (breath, rain, food), provides moral awareness, affords civil government, and restrains evil so that human life and culture is possible. *Special grace* refers to the grace by which God redeems, sanctifies, and glorifies his people. *Prevenient grace* refers to the grace which comes before all human effort or decisions and makes it possible for people to desire salvation and respond in faith.

📖 **7**
page 271
Outline Point I-D-1

[Pelagius taught that] the power to do good resides naturally in the free will itself, apart from any gift of God to human nature, so that by following the example of Christ, the way of virtue is made clear and persons of their own will may abstain from sin. Hence there is a need not for any direct prevenient operation of the Spirit upon the human will in order for it to do good, but merely for the Spirit to operate indirectly through conscience and reason... Between A.D. 411 and 431, no fewer than twenty-four councils faced the question of Pelagianism. It was the burning issue of Augustine's mature life... .The consensual response [of the Church] was further refined at the councils of Ephesus (431) and Orange (529), which held grace to be necessary for all acts pertinent to salvation. "No branch can bear fruit by itself; it must remain in the vine. Neither can you bear fruit unless you remain in me (John 15.4; cf. 1 Cor. 12.3).

~ Thomas C. Oden. *The Transforming Power of Grace.*
Nashville: Abingdon Press, 1993. pp. 110-111.

📖 **8**
page 272
Outline Point I-D-2

Evangelical theology starts with the premise that the formula for salvation is always "by *grace* through *faith*." Make sure that every student understands this basic truth.

📖 9
page 273
Outline Point II

Worship Defined

The principal biblical terms, the Hebrew *saha* and the Greek *proskyneo*, emphasize the act of prostration.

~ E. F. Harrison, "Worship." *Evangelical Dictionary of Theology*. p. 1192.

Worship is responding to God with full recognition of his rightful position as the One who is worthy of absolute adoration, obedience, service, gratitude, and praise.

Ps. 95.6 – Come let us bow down in worship, let us kneel before the Lord our Maker (cf., Lev. 26.1; Deut. 26.10; Ps. 138.2; Matt. 4.9-10).

Some Key Assumptions

The Word basis of worship: we worship the One who is revealed to us.

Apart from the hearing of God's Word we could not worship because we would not know him. He dwells in unapproachable light. Only because he has revealed himself can we respond to him.

John 1.18 – No one has ever seen God, but God the One and Only, who is at the Father's side, has made him known.

The covenant basis of worship: we worship by means of Christ Jesus (Hebrews). Christian worship is distinctive in that it is christocentric. The veil has been torn away. We have direct access to the Father through Christ Jesus. Giving glory to God the Father through him. (Heb. 10.20 – By a new and living way opened up for us through the curtain, that is, his body . . .)

The communal basis of worship: the holy priesthood (worship is always corporate first, individual second).

Heb. 10.25 – Let us not give up meeting together, as some are in the habit of doing, but let us encourage one another – and all the more as you see the Day approaching.

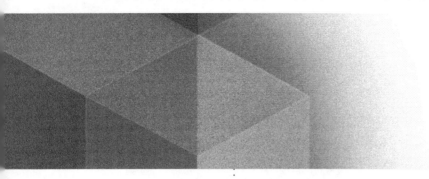

CHRISTIAN MINISTRY

1

📖 **10**
page 273
Outline Point II-B

It has been said that sacraments are like the signature on a check. They are not the same thing as the actual money in the bank or the desire of the person who writes it to see you provided for but they do make those things visible. The signature by itself would be worthless but it serves as a visible sign of what the person is providing and thus is very valuable. Likewise, a sacrament has no value in itself but has great value as the visible sign of God's promise.

📖 **11**
page 273
Outline Point II-B-2

The Catholic Church recognizes seven sacraments: baptism, the Lord's Supper, confirmation, penance, holy orders (ordination), matrimony, and extreme unction (anointing of the seriously ill) in addition to many smaller acts called "sacramentals" (such as "the sign of the cross) which are also believed to confer grace.

📖 **12**
page 274
Outline Point II-C-1

Some Pentecostal, Mennonite, and a few Baptist groups also practice foot washing as an additional ordinance (cf. John 13.14) in addition to baptism and the Lord's Supper.

📖 **13**
page 275
Outline Point III-A-2

The common analogy would be that baptism in the New Testament doesn't automatically save a person any more than being circumcised in the Old Testament automatically saved a person. It was possible to be physically circumcised and yet choose to live as an idolatrous and unbelieving Jew. Circumcision was the sign of the Old Covenant and baptism is the sign of the new. They are both intended to show that a person is genuinely a part of God's chosen people but one must not make the mistake of assuming that baptism automatically makes a person a Christian. This is equally true whether one sees baptism as a sacrament or as an ordinance.

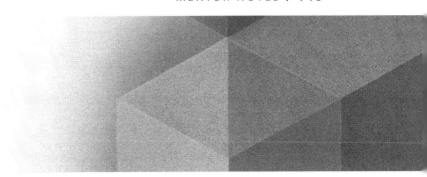

📖 **14**
page 276
Outline Point III-C

In this sense, being baptized is no more optional than it was optional for the Hebrew people to decline eating the Passover and putting the blood on the doorpost. To disobey the command of God was to disassociate oneself from the people of God who were being rescued. The obedience in the Exodus story revealed that a person believed God and was committed to leaving with his people. While an extraordinary circumstance might prevent a person from being baptized (e.g. the thief on the cross) without placing that person's intentions in question, all true believers who have the opportunity to be baptized will do so because they have accepted Christ's lordship and want to obey his commands and be incorporated into his people.

📖 **15**
page 276
Outline Point IV

If students need a resource for practical help on leading a communion service (or a baptism), *Baker's Worship Handbook*, by Paul E. Engle (Grand Rapids, MI: Baker Book House, 1998) offers a number of sample services from a wide variety of Evangelical traditions including both "sacramental" and "ordinance" perspective.

📖 **16**
page 278
Outline Point IV-D-1

Another major difference between Catholic and Protestant theology about the Lord's Supper is the Catholics believe that Christ is sacrificed for sin each time that the Lord's Supper is reenacted. (Protestants refute this on the basis of Hebrews 7.27 and 9.25-26). Unlike Protestants, Catholics also teach that the communion elements (being the actual body and blood of Christ) are worthy of veneration. Catholics and Protestants have made progress in recent years at resolving these differences but differences still remain.

CHRISTIAN MINISTRY

1

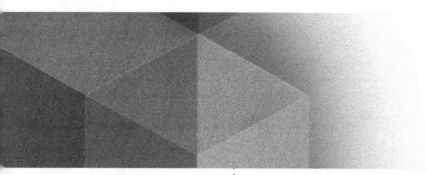

📖 **17**
page 279
Outline Point IV-E-1

It has been held that the substance of bread and wine remain in this sacrament after consecration. But this position cannot be maintained, for in the first place it destroys the reality of this sacrament, which demands that in the sacrament there should be the true body of Christ, which was not there before consecration. . . .And this is done in the sacrament by the power of God, for the whole substance of bread is converted into the whole substance of Christ's body. Hence the conversion is properly called transubstantiation. It is obvious to our sense that after consecration all the accidents of bread and wine remain. And, by divine providence, there is good reason for this. First, because it is not normal for people to eat human flesh and to drink human blood, in fact, they are revolted by this idea. Therefore Christ's flesh and blood are set before us to be taken under the appearances of those things which are of frequent use, namely bread and wine. Secondly, if we ate our Lord under his proper appearance, this sacrament would be ridiculed by unbelievers. Thirdly, in order that, while we take the Lord's body and blood invisibly, this fact may avail toward the merit of Faith.

~ Thomas Aquinas. *Summa Theologiae* (1265).

📖 **18**
page 280
Outline Point IV-E-2

What is true concerning Christ is also true concerning the sacrament. In order for the divinity to dwell in a human body, it is not necessary for the human nature to be transubstantiated and the divinity contained under the accidents of the human nature. Both natures are simply there in their entirety and it is true to say: 'This man is God; this God is man. . . .' In the same way it is not necessary in the sacrament that the bread and wine be transubstantiated and that Christ be contained under their accidents in order that a real body and real blood may be present. But both remain there at the same time, and it is truly said, 'This bread is my body; this wine is my blood,' and vice versa.

~ Martin Luther. *The Babylonian Captivity of the Church* (1520).

"On this we take our stand, and we also believe and teach that in the Supper we eat and take to ourselves Christ's body truly and physically." While [Luther] acknowledged the mystery, he was certain of the fact of Christ's real corporeal presence inasmuch as he had said when he instituted the Supper, "This is my body." If Scripture cannot be taken literally here, it cannot be believed anywhere, Luther held, and we are on the way to "the virtual denial of Christ, God, and everything" (Works, XXXVII, 29, 53).

~ M. E. Osterhaven. Quoting Luther in "Lord's Supper, Views of." *Evangelical Dictionary of Theology.* Grand Rapids: Baker, 1984. p. 655.

📖 **19**
page 283
Student Questions
and Response

In these questions, you will find the focus is upon mastering the data and the facts associated with the claims made in the video. Concentrate on ensuring that the students understand the answers in light of the lesson aims. Make certain that you watch the clock here, covering the questions below and those posed by your students, and watch for any tangents which may lead you from rehearsing the critical facts and main points.

📖 **20**
page 284
Summary of
Key Concepts

Make certain that you distinguish between the Church's response in its worship towards God (worship in terms of its *effect*) and the beauty of the Lord and his character and works in Jesus Christ (worship in terms of its cause). Unfortunately, some discussions of worship have become more focused on the *ways in which we worship* rather than the *reasons why we worship*. While both are important in understanding the Church's vocation as a worshiping priesthood of believers, it is imperative that the focus remain on the God whom we worship, and the clear reason why we are a worshiping community. Only when these concepts are reiterated and kept clear can we rightly consider the ways in which we are to approach God. The *why* of worship must necessarily and understandably precede the *what* and the *how* of worship. This statement ought not to be

CHRISTIAN MINISTRY

1

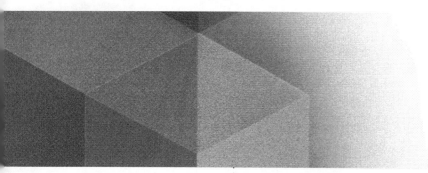

understood as an appeal to belittle the significance of discussions about human responses to God. It is, however, to underscore that worship's significance derives from the understanding that *God is worthy of our obeisance and our obedience*. Discussions of worship should begin and end in a "theocentric" vein (God-centered) not an "anthropocentric" vein (human-centered one).

📖 **21**
page 285
Student Application
and Implications

While there are many individual and personal implications to this teaching on worship, it will be important for you as mentor to help the students retain the corporate nature of the questions and the issues. The tendency to turn the discussion about the Church at worship to "me at worship" is a strong one, and your ability in review and reflection with the students to keep them on the communal implications is important here.

📖 **22**
page 286
Case Studies

These case studies highlight the concern of the nature of worship in our congregations. The need here is to enable your students to understand the general teachings, truths, and principles associated with the Church at worship, and their ability to apply these principles to real-life problems associated with the Church's worship today. Each of the following case studies can be understood through an array of perspectives and principles covered in this lesson. The aim, of course, is not to give the perfect answer in order to clarify the situation or resolved the problem, but to help the students gain skill in addressing particular existential problems and concerns while keeping specific biblical principles in mind. Armed with the truth of the Word and the experience of Christian history and tradition, the students can use their own experience and understandings to help carve new directions to understanding and address these questions. Help them apply different principles to the situations and see how those principles make clear the underlying questions or concerns which need to be addressed.

CHRISTIAN MINISTRY

1

📖 **23**
page 288
Counseling and Prayer

Always encourage the students to not simply study the word of God, making the most of their critical functions, but also to pray fervently over issues, and so exercise their spiritual gifts and capacities. All the issues we face as leaders will require our specific and ongoing intercession, and by emphasizing this in our lessons we train our students to never study the Bible without reference to the wisdom that only God can provide, the kind that will never make us ashamed but will enable us to represent God in the way he desires (James 1.5-8). Admitting that we do not understand something is never a problem to the Lord; God is beyond us and will provide us with wisdom if we search for it with all our hearts, and not simply with all our minds (Prov. 2.1-9). As the writer to the Proverbs suggests, we are never to lean on our own understanding as if we could conjure up solutions because we thought well (Prov. 3.5-6). Train the students, even after the Word has been consulted, to look to God in prayer. It is not prayer or the Word, but prayer alongside the Word that characterized the ministry of the apostles, and should characterize ours (Acts 6.4). Encourage your students to seek the Lord's face in prayer and ask him for specific insights, approaches, and solutions to the issues and concerns they face, both in their personal lives as well as their ministries.

CHRISTIAN MINISTRY

1

Foundations of Christian Leadership
The Christian Leader as Pastor – *Poimenes*

📖 1
page 291
Lesson Introduction

Welcome to the Mentor's Guide for Lesson 2, *Foundations of Christian Leadership: The Christian Leader as Pastor – Poimenes*. The overall focus of this lesson is the critical role that the image of shepherding has for our understanding of the practice of Christian Leadership. The image is significant in every way – our Lord used it often as a beloved image of the kind of relationship he has with his own, and the Apostles adopted this imagery to fill out the nature of the work that Christian leaders do in relationship to the Church.

Even the most cursory look at the imagery of the *shepherd* in Scripture reveals its importance as a metaphor to communicate to us God's meaning of Christian leadership and nurture. A. D. Clarke provides us with a concise summary of some of the more significant images of shepherd in the Scriptures:

> A number of shepherds were chosen to be significant leaders of God's people, namely Joseph (Gen. 37.2; 47.1-4), Moses (Exod. 3.1) and David (1 Sam. 16.11; 17.15; Ps. 78.70-72). God himself is repeatedly described as a shepherd over his people (Gen. 49.24; Ps. 23.1; 28.9; 80.1; Isa. 40.10-11; Ezek. 34; Mic. 2.12; Matt. 25.32-33), and Jesus is the chief shepherd of the sheep (John 10.1-18; Heb. 13.20; 1 Pet. 2.25; 5.4; Rev. 7.17; cf. also Matt. 15.24). Bad shepherds are rebuked for their lack of care for their flock (Zech. 11.4-17), and both Jeremiah and Ezekiel are used by God to chastise those who have been bad shepherds over his people. God himself will gather the flock back into the fold and will appoint new shepherds who will care for it (Jer. 23.1-4; Ezek. 34.23-24). He calls leaders to be shepherds (2 Sam. 5.2; 7.7), and the role of the godly leader is to watch over, care for, feed, and protect the sheep (Jer. 3.15; John 21.15-17; Acts 20.28; 1 Pet. 5.1-3).

> ~ A. D. Clark. "Leadership." *New Dictionary of Biblical Theology*. (electronic ed.). Downers Grove, IL: InterVarsity Press, 2001.

The significance of this image cannot be overestimated, and so your challenge will be to help your students gain a solid understanding of its elements and implications for Christian leadership. To be a Christian leader is to pastor, to shepherd the flock of God or, as Clark puts it, to "watch over, care for, feed, and protect the sheep." Throughout this

2

CHRISTIAN MINISTRY

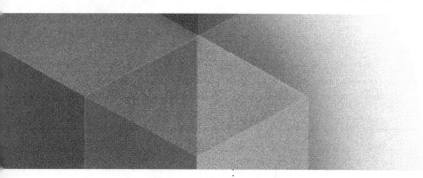

lesson we will explore this image, and weigh its importance and impact on us today as we seek to lead God's people into his fullness.

As usual, your attention to the objectives will enable you to stay focused and on point as you discuss the many-sided nature of the pastoral ministry with your students.

📖 **2**
page 291
Devotion

This devotion focuses on our need to follow the example of our Lord in his role as the Good Shepherd. The image of the shepherd is one of the most beloved and important metaphors to picture forth the kind of care, nurture, and protection involved in leading the people of God. In a real sense this image, although agrarian and not urban, still provides a remarkably powerful image of the kind of devotion God seeks for his leaders.

Actually, the term for "shepherd" is also interchanged with the term "pastor" in the Hebrew Scriptures (cf. Jer. 2.8; 3.15; 10.21; 12.10; 17.16). Often the image of the shepherd is used to picture forth the relationship of the Lord to the people of Israel (Ps. 23.1; 80.1; Isa. 40.11; 44.28; Jer. 25.34, 35; Nah. 3.18). This notion is adopted and expanded in our Lord's attribution of the image of Shepherd to himself, and by the Apostles who employ it of the Lord Jesus as well (John 10.11, 14; Heb. 13.20; 1 Pet. 2.25; 5.4).

This image of the leader's role being compared to a shepherd is both striking and vivid. The responsibility was neither simple nor comfortable. To actually shepherd a flock in a rugged country like Palestine was treacherous and difficult. Read carefully how one scholar summarizes the various dimensions of this task:

> In early morning he led forth the flock from the fold, marching at its head to the spot where they were to be pastured. Here he watched them all day, taking care that none of the sheep strayed, and if any for a time eluded his watch and wandered away from the rest, seeking diligently till he found and brought it back. In those lands sheep require to be supplied regularly with water, and the shepherd for this purpose has to guide them either to some running stream or to wells dug in

CHRISTIAN MINISTRY

2

the wilderness and furnished with troughs. At night he brought the flock home to the fold, counting them as they passed under the rod at the door to assure himself that none were missing. Nor did his labors always end with sunset. Often he had to guard the fold through the dark hours from the attack of wild beasts, or the wily attempts of the prowling thief (see 1 Sam. 17.34).

~ David M. Easton. *Easton's Bible Dictionary.* (electronic ed. of 1897 printing). Oak Harbor, WA: Logos Research Systems, Inc., 1996.

What is important to understand is that the call to pastor is simultaneously a call to be like the Lord Jesus, the one who epitomizes the kind of self-sacrificing care that we must have for his little ones. This call to rigorous and challenging oversight and guardianship presents a perfect picture of what it means to care for the sheep of the Lord. Only when we understand the rigor of this task can we appreciate the kind of connection our Lord made for himself, and the kind of challenge involved for those of us called to care for the people of God.

📖 3
page 313
Ministry Connections

It is apparent from these discussions on the nature of Christian leadership that your students cannot expect others to submit to them *unless they are currently submitting to others right now.* There simply is no way that someone ought to expect God to grant them authority when they refuse to obey and submit to the legitimate authority that the Lord has provided them. This principle is inviolate and constant, and it applies to all in leadership or in development to become a leader. Whether someone merely aspires to the role of Church leadership or presently occupies a position of authority in the Church today, they simply must demonstrate submission in their own lives in order to expect submission. As such, your students must understand the importance of receiving the leaders that God has supplied for them (Eph. 4.7-11; 1 Pet. 5.1-5), honoring them in all the work that they do on behalf of the Church (cf. 1 Tim. 5.17, "Let the elders who rule well be considered worthy of double honor, especially those who labor in preaching and teaching,"). Finally, exhort your students on the importance of the discipline of obedience to leadership (Heb. 13.7-9,

CHRISTIAN MINISTRY

2

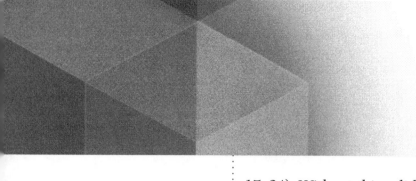

17, 24). Without this solid foundation of honor, respect, and obedience, it will be virtually impossible for them to either understand the role of pastoral ministry, or be in a position to actually pastor another.

Emphasize the importance of submission for pastors, for truly, the flock always belongs to God and never to those who serve it.

📖 4
page 313
Assignments

By the end of the second class session, you ought to emphasize with the students the need for them to have done the spadework and thought out precisely how they intend on carrying out their Ministry Project. Also, by this time, you should have emphasized their selection of the passage they will study for their Exegetical Project. Both will be done with far better thought and excellence the earlier the students begin to think through them and decide what they want to do. Do not fail to emphasize this, for, as in all study, at the end of the course many things become due, and the students will begin to feel the pressure of getting a number of assignments in at the same time. Any way that you can remind them of the need for advanced planning will be wonderfully helpful for them, whether they realize it immediately or not.

Because of this, we do advocate that you consider docking a modest amount of points for late papers, exams, and projects. While the amount may be nominal, your enforcement of your rules will help them to learn to be efficient and on time as they continue in their studies.

LESSON 3

Practicing Christian Leadership
Effective Worship Leading

📖 **1**
page 315
Lesson Introduction

Welcome to the Mentor's Guide for Lesson 3, *Practicing Christian Leadership: Effective Worship Leading – Worship, Word, and Sacrament*. The overall focus of this lesson is on Christian leadership, the kind of leadership that can establish, equip, and empower disciples in the city for ministry. This lesson seeks to highlight the ways in which Christian leaders provide care for the spiritual well-being and welfare of others, those whom they either formally or informally lead in the body of Christ.

Immediately, it would be helpful for you to understand, review, and teach to your students the general outlines of what is involved in Christian leadership as understood formally in the New Testament. There are two designations in the New Testament for leader, generally. The first, "presbyters" or elder (Gk. *presbuteros*), which carries the connotation of someone who is both older and a believer, either for an older man or woman (1 Tim. 5.1, 2). It is used also for both Church leaders (Acts 14.23; 15.2, 4, 6) as well as members of the Sanhedrin (Acts 4.5). This term focuses on the dignity, station, and credibility of the role of Christian leadership. It speaks, likewise of authority and responsibility; elders had authority to distribute the funds of the body for the well-being of others (Acts 11.30), determine issues of doctrine and ethical practice (Acts 15.2-6, 22; 16.2), and to receive updates from the evangelists and apostles on the progress of their work (Acts 20.17; 21.18). They were to be entrusted with authority, respected in their service, and charged with prayer for the sick and those requiring care (1 Tim. 5.17; 1 Pet. 5.1-4; James 5.14).

The second formal sense of leadership has to do with overseers, or bishops (Gk. *episkopos*). This term related to the Christian leader's responsibility to guard or give watch over the flock of God, in the same way that a shepherd watches over his sheep. In like manner, all of the duties of a shepherd are applied to the role of the bishop, to nurture, feed, guard, and protect the flock of God (cf. Acts 20.28; 1 Tim. 3.2; Titus 1.7). When we compare the Scriptures of Acts 20.17, 28 and Titus 1.5, 7 show that the terms for "elder" and "overseer" are used in a way to show that they refer to the same position in the Church. Some have described that *presbuteros* stresses the dignity of Christian leadership and *episkopos* focuses on the work Christian leaders do. This is a helpful

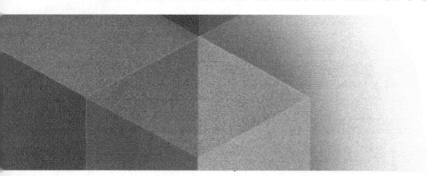

designation thoroughly consistent with the meaning of the terms in Scripture.

For a full listing of the qualifications of these formal offices please refer carefully to 1 Timothy 3.1-7 and Titus 1.5-9. People of the highest moral, spiritual, and theological character are to be appointed to positions of Christian leadership in the Church. The reason for this high character is plain; elders and bishops were charged with leading the flock of the Lord (Acts 20.28), teaching and nurturing them in the Word of God (1 Tim. 3.2), and providing general oversight in the affairs of the community, especially protecting them from the errors and attacks of unscrupulous deceivers and the deceits of the enemy (1 Tim. 5.17; Titus 1.9). The fact that elders are often mentioned as more than one says that we must conceive of Christian leadership as a plurality in the body of Christ; God will raise up a sufficient number of qualified spiritual laborers to care for his people (see Acts 14.23; Phil. 1.1; Titus 1.5). To these two designations we can also add the role of deacons (Gk. *diakonos*), or "servants" or "ministers" whose roles seemed to focus on providing support to the elders, while assuming responsibility for ministering to the material needs of the body (cf. Acts 6.1-6). These leaders were to be people of high character and devotion to the Lord (1 Tim. 3.8-13).

All in all, through elders, bishops, and deacons, the Church of God has been supplied through the grace of God with a remarkable resource of spiritual laborers to protect, feed, and care for the body of Christ.

In the objectives section of the Student Workbook you will notice that these aims are clearly stated, and you ought to emphasize them throughout the lesson, during the discussions and interaction with the students. The more you can highlight the objectives throughout the class period, the better the chances are that they will understand and grasp the magnitude of these objectives. Indeed, the more aware you are of the objectives, the more integrated and helpful the teaching material will be for your students throughout the sessions.

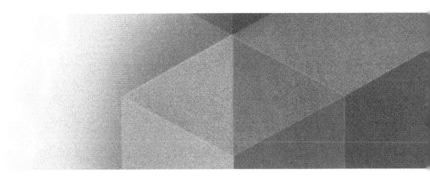

2
page 315
Lesson Objectives

Do not hesitate to discuss these objectives briefly before you enter into the class period. Draw the students' attention to the objectives, for, in a real sense, this is the heart of your educational aim for the class period in this lesson. Everything discussed and done ought to point back to these objectives. Find ways to highlight these at every turn, to reinforce them and reiterate them as you go.

In a real sense, focusing on the objectives gives you a constellation to navigate the flow and content of the class by. Refer to them often with the students, and relate the various points of interest and conversation to them as you lead them.

In all things, the operative principle ought to be what Paul said to Timothy:

> 2 Timothy 2.20-21 – Now in a great house there are not only vessels of gold and silver but also of wood and clay, some for honorable use, some for dishonorable. [21] Therefore, if anyone cleanses himself from what is dishonorable, he will be a vessel for honorable use, set apart as holy, useful to the master of the house, ready for every good work.

All students must be prepared for the work which the Lord may call them to. It is in this spirit that we encourage you to exhort your students to strive for excellence and depth.

3
page 315
Devotion

This devotion focuses on the concept of representation, which is a critical metaphor for all leadership in Scripture, expressed and shown in both the Old and New Testaments. A number of texts highlight this emphasis; notice how each one gives a sense of representation in spiritual leadership:

> 2 Cor. 5.20 – Therefore, we are ambassadors for Christ, God making his appeal through us. We implore you on behalf of Christ, be reconciled to God.

> Job 33.23 – If there be for him an angel, a mediator, one of the thousand, to declare to man what is right for him.

CHRISTIAN MINISTRY

3

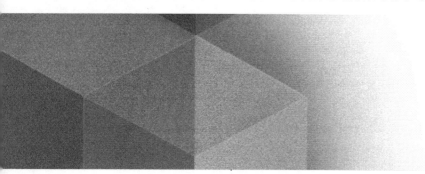

Prov. 13.17 – A wicked messenger falls into trouble, but a faithful envoy brings healing.

Mal. 2.7 – For the lips of a priest should guard knowledge, and people should seek instruction from his mouth, for he is the messenger of the Lord of hosts.

John 20.21 – Jesus said to them again, "Peace be with you. As the Father has sent me, even so I am sending you."

Luke 10.16 – The one who hears you hears me, and the one who rejects you rejects me, and the one who rejects me rejects him who sent me.

Acts 26.17-18 – delivering you from your people and from the Gentiles – to whom I am sending you [18] to open their eyes, so that they may turn from darkness to light and from the power of Satan to God, that they may receive forgiveness of sins and a place among those who are sanctified by faith in me.

2 Cor. 3.6 – who has made us competent to be ministers of a new covenant, not of the letter but of the Spirit. For the letter kills, but the Spirit gives life.

Eph. 6.20 – for which I am an ambassador in chains, that I may declare it boldly, as I ought to speak.

Enabling your students to see that they, in fact, represent the risen and exalted Lord Jesus in their leadership is one of the critical empowering elements of this lesson. What they are engaged in is not merely good efforts or care; they stand in the place of and for the glory of the Lord Jesus, and he himself will reward their faithful obedience in serving the needs of his people. This corresponds directly to the way in which our Lord obeyed the Father, and therefore God highly exalted him (Phil. 2.5-11). In the same way, we honor Christ, and so he will honor us (John 12.24-25). This was applied as well to receiving the apostles' words as Christ's own instruction (cf. 1 Thess. 4.8 – Therefore whoever disregards this, disregards not man but God, who gives his Holy Spirit to you.)

Notice this sense of representation again in the following texts:

Matt. 10.40 – Whoever receives you receives me, and whoever receives me receives him who sent me.

Mark 9.37 – Whoever receives one such child in my name receives me, and whoever receives me, receives not me but him who sent me.

Luke 9.48 – and said to them, "Whoever receives this child in my name receives me, and whoever receives me receives him who sent me. For he who is least among you all is the one who is great."

John 12.44 – And Jesus cried out and said, "Whoever believes in me, believes not in me but in him who sent me."

John 12.48 – The one who rejects me and does not receive my words has a judge; the word that I have spoken will judge him on the last day.

John 13.20 – Truly, truly, I say to you, whoever receives the one I send receives me, and whoever receives me receives the one who sent me.

📖 **4**
page 328
Student Questions
and Response

These questions are designed to ensure that the students understand the critical aims and facts presented in the video. Your role as mentor is to use the questions to review the key concepts and insights presented in the video, as well as draw out the students to see that they understand them as presented.

It will be necessary, of course, for you to gauge your time well, especially if your students are intrigued with the concepts, and want to discuss their implications at length. Your class session and its length should guide you in the kind of freedom you give yourself and your students to interact on the various concerns and issues that emerge from your dialogue.

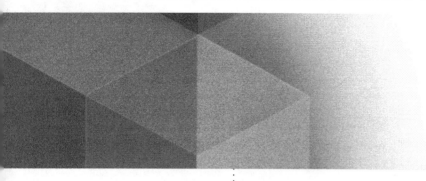

3

CHRISTIAN MINISTRY

📖 **5**
page 329
Summary of
Key Concepts

This section of a lesson offers you an opportunity to review the key concepts of the entire lesson and any other ideas which have emerged in your study of the theme. The statements listed below, therefore, represent the fundamental truths which the students should take away from the materials in this lesson, that is, from the videos and your guided discussion with them. Make sure that these concepts are clearly defined and carefully considered, for their quiz work and exams will be taken from these items directly.

📖 **6**
page 329
Student Application
and Implications

In helping your students think through their own situations, you might want to design some questions or use those provided below as water to "prime the pump" of their interests, so to speak. It is important that you help the students develop habits of critical thinking, the ability to ponder not only what the facts are but also (and more importantly) what the meaning of those facts are in light of their own lives and ministries. So, please see this sections and its questions in the proper light. What is significant here is not that you merely ask the questions written below, but that you, in conversation with your students, start to help them identify that cadre of issues, concerns, questions, and ideas that flow directly from their experience.

Do not hesitate to spend the majority of time on some question that arose from the video, or some special concern that is especially relevant in their ministry context right now. The goal of this section is for you to enable them to think critically and theologically in regards to their own lives and ministry contexts. Again, the questions below are provided as guides and primers, and ought not to be seen as absolute necessities. Pick and choose among them, or come up with your own. The key is relevance now, to their context and to their questions.

📖 **7**

page 333
Assignments

A part of a good classroom situation is that the students are clear regarding their responsibilities for class, that is, that they know all facets of the assignment, that all their questions regarding those assignments are known and answered, and that you as mentor or instructor are prepared to lead them to the next theme and study.

Make certain that the students understand the assignment for next week, especially what they are responsible for in their summaries of the texts they are to read. This is not difficult; the goal is that they would read the material as best as they can and write a few sentences on what they take them to mean. This is a critical intellectual skill for your students to learn, so make sure that you encourage them in this process. Of course, for those students who might find this difficult, assure them of the intent behind this assignment, and emphasize their understanding of the material being the key, not their writing skills. We want to improve their skills, but not at the expense of their encouragement and edification. Nor, however, do we want to sell them short. Strike to find the midpoint between challenge and encouragement here.

3

CHRISTIAN MINISTRY

LESSON
4

The Equipping Ministry
The Ministry of Proclamation – *Kerygma*

📖 1
page 335
Lesson Introduction

Welcome to the Mentor's Guide for Lesson 4, *The Equipping Ministry: The Ministry of Proclamation – Kerygma*. The overall focus of this lesson is to highlight what the role of the Holy Spirit and methods are to effective biblical preaching. At first glance, it would appear that a dependence upon the Holy Spirit and clear presentation methodology would be mutually exclusive; isn't a reliance of the Spirit the mirror-image opposite of reliance on human method? While it will be argued throughout this lesson that the Spirit alone is capable of enabling men and women to understand the truth of the Word of God and apply it to their lives, we will also advocate for shrewdness, diligence, and discipline in the preparation of messages and awareness of sound principles of communication in the delivery of sermons. In all presentation of the Word of God, sincerity is not enough. We endorse the Pauline exhortation that, whatever the gift the Lord has given you (including the Word-oriented gifts of preaching and teaching), do with all your might and sense of excellence and discipline (cf. Rom. 12.4-8).

In this lesson we highlight again the role of divine unction and empowerment both in the delivery and reception of the message of the Word of God. Here, again, it would help for you to read a nicely organized summary of the importance of theology of preaching to Christian leadership development, and K. Runia provides such a summary for us:

> In the Bible, preaching plays a major part. This is true of the OT (cf. Prophecy), but in particular of the NT. One may even say that the NT itself is the result of preaching. Both the gospels and the epistles are fully kerygmatic. Jesus himself continually proclaimed the coming of the kingdom of God. Even more, in his preaching and healing activities the kingdom was already present. In his cross and resurrection God's eschatological act of redemption took place. This is also the reason why after his resurrection and the outpouring of the Spirit Jesus himself is the main content of the apostolic proclamation. It is therefore not surprising to see that the New Testament uses more than thirty verbs to denote the activity of preaching. The apostles, commissioned by the risen Lord, preached this message as the very word of God (cf. 2 Thess. 2.13). The Pauline Epistles frequently use such expressions as 'the word of God' or 'the word of the Lord' or, in an even shorter formula, 'the

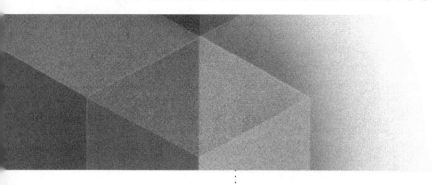

word' (cf. 1 Thess. 1.6, 8; 3.1; Col. 4.3; 2 Tim. 2.9; 4.1; etc.). In all these passages the terms refer to the preached word (cf. TDNT IV, 116). This is also the reason why the word preached by Paul and the others is effective. This efficacy is not due to the talents of the preacher, but the secret lies in the genitive: it is the word of God or of the Lord. In the apostolic message (the emphasis being always on the content) the voice of the living God is being heard.

This emphasis was shared by the Reformers. Both Luther and Calvin were convinced that, when the message of the gospel of Jesus Christ is being proclaimed, God himself is heard by the listeners. In chapter 1 of the Second Helvetic Confession (1566) Heinrich Bullinger, the successor of Zwingli, summarized the position of the Reformers in one terse statement: *Praedicatio verbi Dei est verbum Dei* – the preaching of the word of God is the word of God. In the next sentence he interprets this statement as follows: 'Wherefore when this word of God (=Scripture) is now preached in the church by preachers lawfully called, we believe that the very word of God is proclaimed, and received by the faithful.'

The indispensable condition for true preaching is the faithful proclamation of the message of Scripture. Yet preaching is not a simple repetition of this message. It must also be actualized into the present. If preaching is to be true and relevant, the message of Scripture must be addressed to people in their concrete historical situation. The biblical message may not be adapted to the situation of today, but it must be 'accommodated' (Calvin) to the situation. As in Christ God stooped down to take upon himself our flesh (see Accommodation, Incarnation), so in the preaching of the word the Holy Spirit stoops down to reach people in their situation. The preacher therefore must be an exegete of both Scripture and of his congregation, so that the living word of God for today will be heard at the intersection of text and situation.

~ K. Runia. "Theology of Preaching." *The New Dictionary of Theology*. S. B. Ferguson, ed. (electronic ed.). Downers Grove, IL: InterVarsity Press, 2000. pp. 527-28.

Your goal in this lesson is to convince the students of the absolute necessity of submission to the leading of the Holy Spirit in all proclamation of the Word, *as well as* a disciplined, diligent practice of good principles of communication, especially as they relate to urban culture and urban audiences. We will emphasize throughout this lesson the significance of *culture* in all effective biblical communication, and you should do as Runia says, and help the students become *exegetes of the Scriptures as well as their audience* in order that the Word of God might be applied to their lives as powerfully and potently as possible.

See again the learning objectives listed in the lesson, and as usual, your responsibility as Mentor is to emphasize these concepts throughout the lesson, especially during the discussions and interaction with the students. The more you can highlight the objectives throughout the class period, the better the chances are that they will understand and grasp the magnitude of these objectives.

📖 **2**

page 335
Devotion

This devotion focuses on the need for us to be prepared for the delivery of the Word of God to others, that is, to be aware of *all the factors involved* in the presentation of the Word of Christ to the lost. Paul in 2 Corinthians 4 makes it plain that the devil is a major character in the preaching event, spending time seeking to blind and deceive the hearers in regard to the truth of Christ and his ability to save and transform their lives. Paul is confident, however, that the power of the Lord Jesus can overcome this strategy of deception and blindness, and suggests that the very glory of God shines brilliantly in the face of Jesus Christ, the same Jesus who is the subject of his Gospel preaching.

In many ways, the presentation of the Gospel can be understood in a fundamentally simple way. P. J. H. Adam summarizes this simplicity and presentation in an article of the theology of preaching:

> We can summarize a biblical theology of preaching in these words: God has spoken, It is written, and Preach the word (P. Adam, *Speaking God's Words*, pp. 15-56). God has spoken. The self-revelation of God is always

4

CHRISTIAN MINISTRY

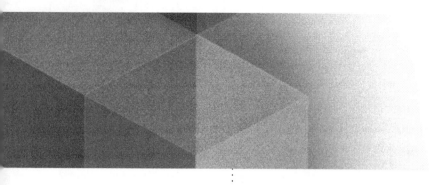

either expressed or explained through words. It is by the words which *God has spoken* that we know who he is, that he has made the universe, and the meaning of his works, his saving acts. It is by these words that we know of the identity and significance of his Son Jesus, of his plan of salvation, and of the gospel. It is by these words that we know how we should respond to God's grace with the obedience of faith, and look forward to the return of Christ and the consummation of God's Kingdom. God has accommodated himself to us and condescended to speak in human language, with perfectly true words, so that we can respond to him in faith as we hear his voice. When God is present, he is present to speak. Whereas he once spoke on earth, he now warns us from heaven (Heb. 12.25).

The idea of God's revelation as "speaking" or "words" is so powerful that it is used as metaphor for God's self-revelation in his Son. So in Hebrews 1 we read that "In the past God spoke . . . at many times and in various ways by the prophets, but in these last days he has spoken to us by his Son"; Paul writes of Jesus that he "preached peace"; and John describes Jesus as "the Word." (Heb. 1.1-2; Eph. 2.17; John 1.1, NIV). God uses words to reveal the Word.

It is written. When God has spoken he has sometimes also caused the words to be recorded for future generations. Throughout the Bible we see him doing this. Moses not only speaks to the people of Israel the words that God has spoken, he also writes them down, so that later generations, who are constituted as the people of God by the same saving acts, can know that he is in a covenant relationship with them. Moses' sermons on the plains of Moab are written down, not only for the immediate hearers, but also for the subsequent generations of God's people. When these ancient writings are rediscovered, read, and obeyed, as in the times of Josiah and Ezra, there is revival. God's words were also written down for us "on whom the fulfilment of the ages has come" (1 Cor. 10.11).

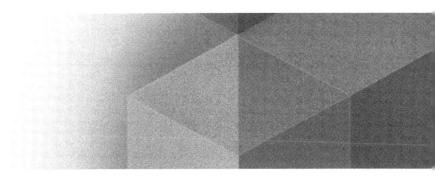

As we become part of the people of God we inherit these promises, covenants, and warnings. In NT times, some of the teaching of Jesus and his followers was written down for the benefit not only of the original readers but also of subsequent generations of God's people. All these words are preserved, or inscripturated, for God's people who live in the last days, which began with Jesus' first coming and will end with his return. As God's saving acts are complete, so also is the verbal revelation that explains them.

Preach the word. The call to preach the word is heard throughout the Bible in many different ways. Abraham as a prophet is to teach his household, and Moses the prophet is to speak, write and read the words of God for the people of God. The priests of the old covenant have the duty of teaching the law given through Moses, and prophets apply the law to their own generation. Wise men and women teach others the way of wisdom; the disciples of Christ preach the Kingdom of God; apostles, pastors and teachers speak the truth in order to bring people to faith in Christ, and to present them mature in Christ. The great need in the post-apostolic church is for teachers, who can teach the truth and refute error. Ordinary believers have the responsibility of encouraging one another with God's words (1 Thess. 4.18); as they do so "the word of Christ" dwells richly among them (Col. 3.16) and this mutual encouragement is God's remedy for the deceitfulness of sin (Heb. 3.13). It is therefore unsurprising that Paul instructs Timothy to preach the word (2 Tim. 4.2).

~ P. J. H. Adam. "Preaching and Biblical Theology."
The New Dictionary of Biblical Theology. T. D. Alexander, ed. (electronic ed.).
Downers Grove, IL: InterVarsity Press, 2001.

Challenge your students to the unbelievable privilege and sobering responsibility they have to preach with clarity, boldness, and without equivocation the Word of the living God. This is their duty, their privilege, and their unswerving responsibility.

CHRISTIAN MINISTRY

4

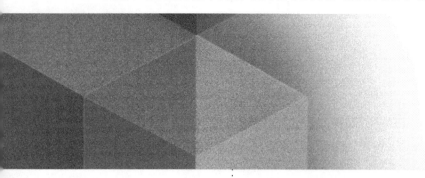

📖 **3**

page 357
Counseling and Prayer

Do not consider it an overly familiar or unnecessary thing to ask the students if they need prayer for someone or something connected to the ideas and truths presented in the lesson. Prayer is a wonderfully practical and helpful way to apply truth; by taking specific needs to God in light of a truth, the students can solidify those ideas in their soul, and receive back from the Lord the answers they need in order to be sustained in the midst of their ministries.

Always emphasize for the students the need for them not merely to *study the truths of God* but to flesh them out in every area of their lives. Indeed, prayer is fundamental to the application of truth in the life of a disciple, and especially in the life of the emerging leader of the Lord and his Church.

Of course, everything is somehow dependent on the amount of time you have in your session, and how you have organized it. Still, prayer is a forceful and potent part of any spiritual encounter and teaching, and if you can, it should always have its place, even if it is a short summary prayer of what God has taught us, and a determination to live out its implications as the Holy Spirit teaches us.

4

CHRISTIAN MINISTRY

Urban Mission

Foundations for Christian Mission
The Vision and Biblical Foundation for Christian Mission

📖 1
page 367
Lesson Introduction

Welcome to the Mentor's Guide for Lesson 1, *Foundations for Christian Mission: The Vision and Biblical Foundation for Christian Mission*. The overall focus of this lesson will be to trace the idea of the story of the divine romance and the war of the spheres as two major motifs of the Scriptures which give a full and helpful sense to our understanding of mission. The overall concept of this lesson is that mission can never be reduced to a kind of evangelism, a method of urban ministry, or a set of services to meet the needs of others. Mission includes these and other varieties of witness and good works, but mission is essentially an extension of the divine drama, romance, war, and promise. We are arguing that true missiology begins with the Scriptures' story of God and his people, God and his creation, and from this secure vantage point, then begins to shape, impact, and direct our missional activities and burdens. Mission that begins with human effort is simply not biblical, in any real sense. In order for mission to be inspired by the Lord it must begin with the Lord's purpose, heart, and working, that redemptive action that culminates in the person and ministry of Jesus of Nazareth. Anything less is not true mission at all.

In a real sense, to understand mission (or any other major field of theology and missiology) is to learn the inspired writers' use of image, metaphor, symbol, and story. Through the inspired use of the imagination, the biblical authors made known to us the plan and purpose of God. Our ability to follow their thinking and rationale will not be possible if we ignore the power of the Christian (and biblically informed) use of the imagination. C. Seerveld makes this point clear:

> A biblically Christian conception of imagination will distinguish imagining from perceptual error, from imaging and from being an oracle of truth. Imaginative human activity is quite distinct from sensing or thinking but is also a bona fide activity interrelated with all human functioning. Imagining is a gift of God with which humans make-believe things. With imagining ability one pretends and acts 'as if' this is that (e.g. God is a rock, Isa. 17.10; Christ is a bridegroom, Matt. 25.1-13). Human imagination is the source of metaphorical knowledge and the playfulness so important to anyone's style of life. Imagination is meant to be an elementary, important, residual moment in everything God's

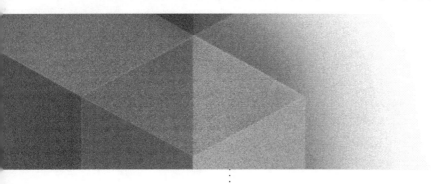

adopted children do. Imagination becomes a curse only if it becomes an exercise in vanity.

~ C. Seerveld. "Imagination." *The New Dictionary of Theology.*
S. B. Ferguson, ed. (electronic ed.). Downers Grove, IL: InterVarsity Press, 2000. p. 331.

Indeed, the only way to get at the *stuff* of mission is through the motifs: God is the bridegroom who is wooing to himself a people which will be his bride and co-regent throughout the endless ages, and God is a warrior who will once and for all defeat the devil, death, and the effects of the curse to usher in a new reign of righteousness and peace.

The motif of the bride and bridegroom is prominent in both the Old and New Testaments. In Scripture, the marriage relation is used often to make sense of God's relationship to his people. Israel is pictured as the unfaithful wife of Yahweh God in Hosea, the wife he is determined to restore to full love and faithfulness in the future Kingdom. This same vision is used to lay out the deep intimacy and affection between Christ and the Church in the New Testament, with the exception that the Lord himself through direct influence and the apostolic ministry is preparing the Church as a virgin bride waiting the coming of her heavenly bridegroom (2 Cor. 11.2). John the Baptist is the Lord's "friend of the bridegroom," analogous to our "best man" today, who prepared the way of the Lord (cf. John 3.29). Jesus made mention of this bridal imagery in his kingdom teaching (cf. Matt. 22.1-14; 25.1-13), and it was used throughout the apostolic instruction and prophetic vision (2 Cor. 11.2; Eph. 5.22-24; Rev. 21.2, 9; 22.17).

Likewise, the Lord as divine warrior is the one who comes to crush the head of the serpent, as mentioned in the *protoevangelium* of Genesis 3.15. Every dimension of the life and ministry of Christ can be understood in the framework of him acting as the divine Son of Man charged with the task to defeat the enemies of God and usher in the reign of God with joy and power. For instance, Leland Ryken summarizes Paul's Christology in these terms, using the divine warrior motif as the organizing principle to comprehend it:

Thus Paul could later look back on the death, resurrection and ascension of Jesus Christ in the light of divine warrior imagery. For

instance, in Colossians 2.13-15 he culminates his argument with divine warrior language: "And having disarmed the powers and authorities, he made a public spectacle of them, triumphing over them by the cross" (Col. 2.15 NIV). In Ephesians 4.8 he cites an OT divine warrior hymn (Ps. 68) and so casts the ascension as a triumphal parade: "When he ascended on high, he led captives in his train and gave gifts to men." (NIV) Thus the divine warrior theme is pressed into service in the NT to describe Jesus' victory over Satan on the cross. Though Satan was defeated, the NT also understands that for a time he is still able to cause great distress. The period of time between the cross and Christ's return is the time between the battle that secured the ultimate victory and the final defeat and cessation of hostility. In the meantime the battle continues, and the church is called upon to wage war against God's enemies just as Israel was God's army in the OT. The difference is that the church's weapons are spiritual, not physical (cf. Eph. 6.10-20).

~ Leland Ryken. *The Dictionary of Biblical Imagery.* (electronic ed.). Downers Grove, IL: InterVarsity Press, 2000. p 213.

Your task in this lesson is to help the students come to grips with these motifs as used by the biblical authors, and to employ them as a *lens to enable you to gain a fresh perspective on the nature of Christian mission viewed through them.* This habit of mind, this mode of interpretation is dramatically helpful in filling out the richness and power of Christian mission today, and to protect it from being reduced to mere technical methodology and rules of practice. Help your students catch the *feeling* of these metaphors and images, the joy of the wedding feast, and the celebration of the defeated enemy. Images are communicated not just for data's sake, but for the sake of the heart and the soul; enable your students to think clearly, but also work to help them feel deeply through these images, for that is why the Lord gave them to us.

Please notice again the objectives below, and recall the way in which they play a central role in every facet of classroom instruction. Again, one of your key responsibilities as Mentor is to emphasize these concepts throughout the lesson, especially during the discussions and interaction with the students. The more you can highlight the objectives

throughout the class period, the better the chances are that they will understand and grasp the magnitude of these objectives.

📖 **2**
page 368
Devotion

This devotion focuses on the idea of the divine romance, with a focus on the marriage supper of the Lamb mentioned in Revelation 19. The idea of marriage as a way of communicating the relationship of God to his people, and the invitation to all to actually come and become a part of that company which constitutes the bride of Christ is a major theme in biblical revelation. R. C. Ortlund, Jr. speaks to this image of Christ as bridegroom and husband to the people of God, the Church, at the consummation of all things mentioned in the great final text of Revelation. Commenting on the scenes provided in heaven after the destruction of the great whore, Babylon, Ortlund suggest that:

> After Babylon, the 'great whore who corrupted the earth with her fornication' (Rev. 19.2), has been judged by God, the victorious saints rejoice that 'the marriage of the Lamb has come, and his bride has made herself ready' (Rev. 19.7). It is granted to her to be clothed with 'fine linen, bright and pure', which is the righteous deeds of the saints (Rev. 19.8). The Husband of the bride presents the church to himself in splendor, without a spot or wrinkle or anything of the kind (cf. Eph. 5.26-27). The antitypical reality finally appears as the new Jerusalem comes down out of heaven from God, prepared as a bride adorned for her husband (Rev. 21.2). There will be no human marriages in heaven (Mark 12.25), for heaven will be the marriage. It is difficult to discuss this without using more lofty prose, as Jonathan Edwards illustrates (*Works* [Edinburgh, 1979 reprint], vol. 2, p. 22): *Then the church shall be brought to the full enjoyment of her bridegroom, having all tears wiped away from her eyes; and there shall be no more distance or absence. She shall then be brought to the entertainments of an eternal wedding-feast, and to dwell for ever with her bridegroom; yea, to dwell eternally in his embraces. Then Christ will give her his loves; and she shall drink her fill, yea, she shall swim in the ocean of his love.* To sum up: the overall pattern of biblical teaching on marriage discloses typological symmetry from Genesis

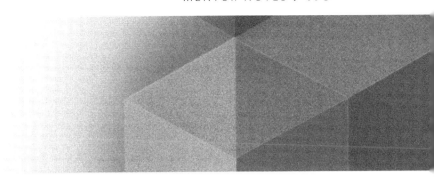

to Revelation, as the 'one-flesh-ness' of human marriage, sacred but provisional, points forward and upward to the eternal spiritual union of Christ with his bride, the church. The symbolism inherent in earthly marriage lends the relationship greater dignity; its significance goes beyond the human and temporal to the divine and eternal.

~ R. C. Ortlund, Jr. "Marriage." *The New Dictionary of Biblical Theology.*
T. D. Alexander, ed. (electronic ed.). Downers Grove, IL: InterVarsity Press, 2000.

Here Ortlund rightly and concisely summarizes the power of the marital imagery to get at the dignity and majesty of the divine marriage, the result of the sacred romance that God has been cultivating with his people since the beginning of time. What Jonathan Edwards refers to as a "eternal wedding feast", and what Ortlund refers to as a "eternal spiritual union" is the referent behind the marriage metaphor. However we are to understand this striking metaphor, we know that the people of God will in fact enjoy intimacy forever with the Lord, and that this relationship is typified in the romance and marriage of earthly wedlock. We get at the depth of the relationship through the symbol, not in spite of it. God invites us to ponder the meaning of the relationship *in the light* of the symbol, and, by doing so, we will come to appreciate at new levels the significance of our union with Christ as a member of his body, the Church.

📖 3
*page 394
Case Studies*

These case studies (as all of them in this lesson reflect) are designed to help the students grapple with issues that either came from real situations, or are fictions based upon situations that informed them. In one sense, the case studies offer the students an opportunity to apply directly and powerfully their insights on the material, and to experiment in the kind of thinking necessary to take truth from a theoretical environment to a practical one. Spend good time with the students hammering out the issues that these studies represent, and remind the students of their purpose in their overall learning environment.

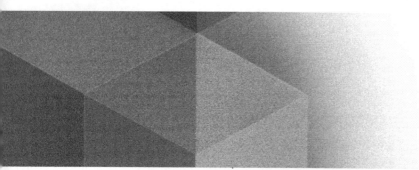

4
page 397
Counseling and Prayer

Prayer is critical to every dimension of learning, growing, applying, and responding to the truth of God. In prayer, both you and your students have an opportunity to get God's direct instruction and leading regarding both the meaning and application of the material.

So, as you enter into a time of prayer with the students, never consider it as something that must be dispensed with quickly, something that can be ignored altogether. Do not treat it as an overly familiar or unnecessary thing; always ask the students if they have any specific requests, whether or not they are connected to the ideas and truths presented in the lesson. Show by your example and attitude that prayer is significant, a wonderfully practical and helpful way to apply truth. Remind them that by taking their specific needs to God in light of a truth, the Lord will both solidify those ideas in their lives, and provide them with specific opportunities to apply them in their ministries.

Of course, everything is somehow dependent on the amount of time you have in your session, and how you have organized it. Still, prayer is a forceful and potent part of any spiritual encounter and teaching, and if you can, it should always have its place, even if it is a short summary prayer of what God has taught us, and a determination to live out its implications as the Holy Spirit teaches us.

LESSON
2

Evangelism and Spiritual Warfare
Binding of the Strong Man

📖 1
page 401
Lesson Introduction

Welcome to the Mentor's Guide for Lesson 2, *Evangelism and Spiritual Warfare: Spiritual Warfare – Binding of the Strong Man*. The overall focus of this lesson is to provide the students with a clear understanding of the knowledge and practice of evangelism and spiritual warfare in the urban context. The focus is on evangelism; the emphasis on spiritual warfare is connected to how evangelism is essentially deliverance from the power of Satan and the dominion of sin and its effects. This is important to recognize, especially because of the limited time we have to cover issues of such great significance and breadth.

Notice in the "Lesson Objectives" section that these aims are clearly stated, and you ought to emphasize them throughout the lesson and during the discussions and interaction with the students. The more you can highlight the objectives throughout the class period, the better the chances are that they will understand and grasp the magnitude of these objectives. *Use the objectives to both teach and review the content of the lesson itself.*

📖 2
page 401
Lesson Objectives

Do not hesitate to discuss these objectives briefly before you enter into the class period. *The more you concentrate upon the actual lesson objectives, the better it will be for your students. This concentration also gives you practical "hooks" on which to hang various facts, data, and ideas that come up in the course of discussion.* Draw the students' attention to the objectives, for, in a real sense, this is the heart of your educational aim for the class period in this lesson. Everything discussed and done ought to point back to these objectives. Find ways to highlight these at every turn, to reinforce them and reiterate them as you go.

📖 3
page 401
Devotion

This devotion focuses on the Lord Jesus' willingness to humble himself in order to become like us. This is a prominent theme of the Scriptures (cf. Matt. 11.29; 20.26-28; Luke 22.27; John 13.14; Acts 10.38; Acts 20.35; Rom. 14.15; 15.3-5; 1 Cor. 10.33-11.1; Eph. 5.2; 1 Pet. 2.21; 4.1; 1 John 2.6). The humility of Jesus lies at the core of all ministry, mission, and outreach. In all that we are and do, we are to imitate the self-forgetful Spirit of our Lord Yeshua who was so willing to pour out his very life for

URBAN MISSION

2

the sake of others. Jesus can empathize with us in infinite ways because he shares our very nature. The Lord Jesus is, quite literally, our very kin, and as such, can sympathize with us in every dimension of our weakness and need.

Evangelism and spiritual warfare are possible because our Lord is one of us, going with us, feeling with us, and is literally there with us (Matt. 18.20; 28.20).

📖 **4**
page 402
Contact

The purpose of contacts in your lesson is to intersect the attention and interests of your students with the subject matter about to be analyzed, discussed, and engaged. It is to awaken in their minds and motives the kinds of questions that will make a study of the material to come necessary and helpful. These contacts are for your suggesting and shaping; if you can think of situations, events, challenges, or realities that may be more on target for the students, please employ them. These are given to help you introduce the subject matter for the session by preparing the students psychologically and mentally for their learning experience.

📖 **5**
page 403
Summary

This lesson concentrates upon the *solution that salvation provides*, which in fact remedies the problem. Right from the beginning you see that salvation is defined in terms of deliverance from the power of the devil and the effects of the Curse, and therefore, evangelism, as the proclamation and demonstration of this deliverance, is at its very heart *spiritual warfare*. Every time a person receives the Lord, violence is taking place in the spiritual realm.

Note this text in Luke:

> Luke 11.17-23 – But he, knowing their thoughts, said to them, "Every kingdom divided against itself is laid waste, and a divided household falls. [18] And if Satan also is divided against himself, how will his kingdom stand? For you say that I cast out demons by Beelzebul. [19] And if I cast out demons by Beelzebul, by whom do your sons cast them out? Therefore they will be your judges. [20] But if it is by the

finger of God that I cast out demons, then the kingdom of God has come upon you. [21] When a strong man, fully armed, guards his own palace, his goods are safe; [22] but when one stronger than he attacks him and overcomes him, he takes away his armor in which he trusted and divides his spoil. [23] Whoever is not with me is against me, and whoever does not gather with me scatters."

📖 **6**
page 409
Summary of
Key Concepts

Listed in this section are the fundamental truths (i.e., the objectives) written in sentence form which the students should have received from this lesson, that is, from the videos and your guided discussion with them. Make sure that these concepts are clearly defined and carefully considered, for their quiz work and exams will be taken directly from these items.

It is imperative that you make sure that the students grasp both the fact of the concepts as well as some of their most significant consequents. In other words, this summary represents the core of what you want the students to grasp out of the lesson, and the substance of the ideas with which they will be tested.

📖 **7**
page 410
Student Application
and Implications

This is where you must do the majority of your own materials, dialogue, suggestions, and additions to the lesson. Helping the students consider options, implications, and ramifications of the teaching is arguably the most important part of the mentor's role in this guided communal learning set.

In helping your students think through their own situations, you might want to design some questions or use those provided below as water to "prime the pump" of their interests, so to speak. What is significant here is not the questions written below, but for you, in conversation with your students, to settle on a cadre of issues, concerns, questions, and ideas that flow directly from their experience, and relate to their lives and ministries. Do not hesitate to spend the majority of time on some question that arose from the video, or some special concern that is especially relevant in their ministry context right now. The goal of this

section is for you to enable them to think critically and theologically in regards to their own lives and ministry contexts. Again, the questions below are provided as guides and primers, and ought not to be seen as absolute necessities. Pick and choose from among them, or come up with your own. The key is relevance, now, to their context and to their questions.

8
page 411
Case Studies

Case studies are designed to pose a real or invented situation in which the actual principles and concepts of the lesson are on display in real or virtual-world environments. The focus here is on wisdom, gaining the ability to wrestle with a actual principle of Scripture in a setting that is not necessarily clear, that demands both knowledge and reflection, and encourages the students to actually apply the teaching as leaders in a setting that has real consequences. Because of this, do not try to make it appear as if there is a single response that is acceptable within the various case studies. Of course, where such an application is present, please emphasize it. However, since most of the case studies allow for a number of "right answers," the goal here is to enable the students to use their spiritual and intellectual gifts to propose "possible ways out" of the dilemma or issues they are facing.

9
page 413
Assignments

Make certain that the students understand the assignment for next week, especially the written piece. This is not difficult; the goal is that they would read the material as best as they can and write a few sentences on what they take them to mean. This is a critical intellectual skill for your students to learn, so make sure that you encourage them in this process.

As a curriculum, however, for those students whose reading level finds these materials challenging or impossible, try to find alternatives for them. Have students share with one another, or give a brief summary of the key lessons of the assignment after the students have handed in their reading assignment sheets.

However you do this, our most fundamental belief is that literacy is not the standard of Christian leadership, but calling, gifting, and power. Help your students, don't frustrate them with these assignments.

Of course, for those students who might find this difficult, assure them of the intent behind this assignment, and emphasize their understanding of the material being the key, not their writing skills. We want to improve their skills, but not at the expense of their encouragement and edification. Nor, however, do we want to sell them short. Strike to find the midpoint between challenge and encouragement here.

Focus on Reproduction
Church Growth – Reproducing in Number and Quality

page 415
Lesson Introduction

1 Welcome to the Mentor's Guide for Lesson 3, *Focus on Reproduction: Church Growth – Reproducing in Number and Quality*. The overall focus of this lesson is to equip your students with an understanding of evangelism, discipleship, and church planting as it relates to the urban community. If urban anthropologists are correct, within the next 20-25 years, every person in three will be an urban-slum dweller! For the first time in human history, more people live in cities than in rural or agrarian areas; missions in the 21st century will, of necessity, be urban mission. The argument of this lesson is that the fastest, most effective, and most fruitful form of spiritual reproduction is urban cross-cultural church planting. Your role in this lesson is to challenge your students to prepare themselves for a new wave of ministry and missions, to become a part of that cadre of urban workers who, if they yield themselves to God with new abandon and focus, can impact, even transform thousands of communities as they go forward in mission, in the power of the Holy Spirit, with the message of Christ, for the glory of God the Father.

The lessons are structured carefully to walk your students through the process of planting churches in the urban community. In lesson one, we begin our study with the subject, *Church Growth, Reproducing in Number and Quality*. Here we affirm the single most critical concept in understanding mission in the city: the lordship of Jesus Christ. As risen Lord and God's Anointed Messiah, Jesus has been exalted to the position of head over all things to the Church and Lord of the harvest. In lesson two, *Planting Urban Churches*, Sowing we introduce the important concept of *oikos* in urban evangelism. Here we show how an *oikos* is that web of common kinship relationships, friendships, and associations that make up a person's larger social circle. Beginning with an outline of *oikos* in the NT, we then explore the meaning of this critical idea for urban cross-cultural evangelism. In lesson three we further outline the second main phase of church planting, *Equipping*, through the idea of *follow-up*, or incorporating new disciples into the Church. Arguing that the Church is God's means of bringing new Christians to maturity, we provide key elements and tips in the practice of following up new believers in Christ. In this lesson we will also look closely at the practice of discipling growing believers. Finally, in lesson four we consider our role in helping new churches progress toward independence through Empowerment,

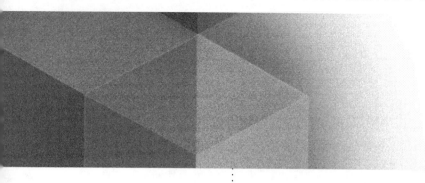

and the final phase of urban church planting: transition. We will define the purpose, plan, and perspectives related to empowering through four biblical aspects of godly urban church leadership. Without a doubt, godly, servant leadership is critical to ensure a dynamic growing church in the city.

Throughout these lessons it will be important for you to emphasize and draw the student's attention to the objectives. Determine right away to emphasize them throughout the lesson, in every part and dimension, and especially during the discussions and interaction with the students. The more you can highlight the objectives throughout the class period, the better the chances are that they will understand and grasp the magnitude of these objectives.

📖 **2**
page 415
Lesson Objectives

Do not hesitate to discuss these objectives briefly before you enter into the class period. Draw the students' attention to the objectives, for, in a real sense, this is the heart of your educational aim for the class period in this lesson. Everything discussed and done ought to point back to these objectives. Find ways to highlight these at every turn, to reinforce them and reiterate them as you go.

📖 **3**
page 415
Devotion

This devotion focuses on the significance of the Great Commission to the Apostles, and the way in which they took this calling seriously, even willing to risk persecution, rejection, and death in order to fulfill it. In a real sense this devotion is on the Great Commission itself, and a nice summary from J. B. Green may be helpful as you orient the students to the heart of Christian mission, which is Jesus' command to go and make disciples of all nations.

> Through the Great Commission of Matthew 28.16-20 Jesus focuses his followers on the ongoing importance of discipleship through the ages. . . Jesus committed his earthly ministry to "making disciples" within Israel (cf. John 4.1), and he commissioned his disciples to

3

URBAN MISSION

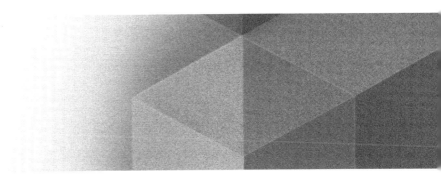

"make disciples" among the nations (Matt. 28.16-20; see Gentiles). The obvious meaning of "making disciples" is to proclaim the gospel message among those who have not yet received forgiveness of sins (Luke 24.46-47; John 20.21; see Forgiveness of Sins). The command finds remarkable verbal fulfillment in the activities of the early Church (e.g., Acts 14.21), where disciples went from Jerusalem to Judea, to Samaria (see Samaritans), to the ends of the earth proclaiming the message of Jesus and making disciples. In the early Church to believe in the gospel message was to become a disciple (cf. Acts 4.32 with 6.2). The injunction of the Great Commission is given at least to the eleven remaining disciples (cf. Matt. 28.16), but in their own role as disciples they are paradigms for all disciples. As Jesus addresses the disciples and commands them to "make disciples of all the nations," Jesus is telling them to continue the work he began with them.

~ J. B. Green. *Dictionary of Jesus and the Gospels.* (electronic ed.) Downers Grove, IL: InterVarsity, 1997. p. 188.

This challenge to the original Apostles is likewise a clarion call of the Lord to the entire generation of Christians in this age to go to the ends of the earth and testify to every people the good news of the Gospel. The Apostles reveal in this passage their uncompromising commitment to be faithful to the Commission, regardless of the opposition, whatever price that must be paid. This is where urban mission and ministry begins: an unconditional availability to do the will of Christ, whatever it takes.

📖 **4**

page 417
Contact

Pay careful attention to the contact sections in these lessons. These portions are specifically designed to "prime the intellectual and spiritual pumps" of your students, to get them ready to consider the biblical content of the lesson, and the corollary implications connected to that content. Be careful that you guide your time well in your use of the contact information; although the incidents and ideas covered are intriguing, they can take a large amount of your lesson time, depending on how you have allocated your time for the lesson.

3

URBAN MISSION

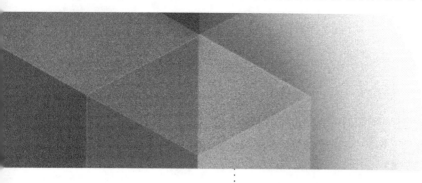

3

📖 **5**
page 433
Summary of
Key Concepts

This section highlights the fundamental truths written in sentence form which the students should have received from this lesson, that is, from the videos and your guided discussion with them. Your aim should be to help your students come to understand the critical principles in proverb form, in a simple, declarative statement that allows them to summarize the material and pass it along to others.

The purpose of the study is to get to the "nuggets," those key principles of truth that they can evaluate, apply, and share in their lives and ministries. It is never a waste of time to make certain that the students are understanding the underlying truths which run through the material. Often, our ability to help our students grapple with these concepts will determine whether or not they are able to *use these truths later*, in their personal edification, their teaching and preaching, and their discipling of others. So, make sure that these concepts are clearly defined and carefully considered, for their quiz work and exams will be taken from these items directly.

📖 **6**
page 434
Student Application
and Implications

While the first part of the lesson concentrates on the need for the students to *master the concepts in the material*, from this moment on the focus is on helping your students *master their own applications in their personal lives*. In other words, students need at least two modes of reflection as they go through the lesson. The first mode is intellectual and dialogical, and focuses on their ability to wrestle with difficult concepts to gain a sense of what the Scriptures actually teach on a particular subject. This mode is *critical*.

However, there is another mode, equally important, which has an entirely different focus. This second mode is personal and spiritual, and focuses on their ability to evaluate the meaning of the truths they have learned relative to their own life applications and ministries. This mode is primarily *creative*.

In light of these ideas, it will always be important at some time in the lesson to shift gears, so to speak, and enable the students to begin to think through their own situations with a greater focus and deliberation. The questions in this section are always designed to be "kindling" to ignite their own fires of inquiry, so to speak. What is

significant here is not that they answer *the particular questions written below*, but that they engage the concepts in such a way that they turn their attention to their *evaluation* and *application* of the issues and themes to their own lives and ministries.

In your conversation with your students, seek to help them settle on a cadre of issues, concerns, questions, and ideas that flow directly from their experience, and relate to their lives and ministries. Do not hesitate to spend the majority of time on some question that arose from the video, or some special concern that is especially relevant in their ministry context right now. The goal of this section is for you to enable them to think critically and theologically in regards to their own lives and ministry contexts. Again, the questions below are provided as guides and primers, and ought not to be seen as absolute necessities. Pick and choose among them, or come up with your own. The key is relevance now, to their context and to their questions.

📖 7

page 435
Case Studies

The case studies function somewhat like the "contact" sections above, with one major difference. Whereas the Contact section was given to help *introduce* your students to the ideas and issues covered in the lesson, the *Case Studies* are actual or probable events designed to help your students show that they can apply the truths in the context of real or probable life situations. Often they are based on true stories, and all the time they reflect the complexity and difficulty of ministering in urban communities.

A large part of the case study section is your ability to help the students become *wise in their application of the truth to particular situations*. Hopefully, your students will be able to apply biblical wisdom to these studies. In general, a three fold approach is helpful:

1. Make sure that the students understand the facts of the situation.

2. After the facts are clear, help your students determine what insights and principles apply to the situation, and how many right answers are possible in the situation.

3

URBAN MISSION

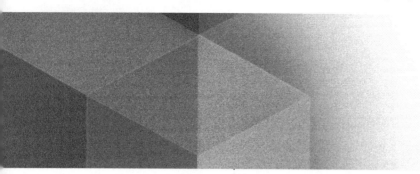

3. Have them actually select solutions to the situations, or approaches they would take, given the insight into the situation and the biblical principles that apply.

This kind of reflection can help your students move from simply consideration of the truth, to its more fundamental application to their own lives and to the life situations of others.

📖 **8**

page 436
Restatement of the
Lesson's Thesis

This section again gives you the right to "pile-drive" the truths one final time into the hearts and minds of the students before you end the lesson.

Lest you think that this kind of approach is overkill, consider the following Scriptures:

Phil. 3.1 – Finally, my brothers, rejoice in the Lord. To write the same things to you is no trouble to me and is safe for you.

2 Pet. 1.12-15 – Therefore I intend always to remind you of these qualities, though you know them and are established in the truth that you have. [13] I think it right, as long as I am in this body, to stir you up by way of reminder, [14] since I know that the putting off of my body will be soon, as our Lord Jesus Christ made clear to me. [15] And I will make every effort so that after my departure you may be able at any time to recall these things.

2 Pet. 3.1 – This is now the second letter that I am writing to you, beloved. In both of them I am stirring up your sincere mind by way of reminder.

2 Tim. 1.6 – For this reason I remind you to fan into flame the gift of God, which is in you through the laying on of my hands.

The ministry of "reminding" is one of the key ministries that the godly teacher can do. Do not hesitate to reiterate the fundamental truths at every turn. You will ensure that the students make these truths their very own.

📖 **9**
page 438
Counseling and Prayer

Seek to make your times of study a time of *spiritual refreshment and awakening* as much as it is a time of *reflection and dialogue on the truth.* If at all possible, structure your time in such a way that you can allow for prayer for the students, and encourage the same in their lives. Prayer has profound power to intermingle with your teaching and produce fruit in their lives with powerful effect. The Lord is willing to help them grow to become more like his Son, and be as effective as they need to be as they learn and apply these truths.

📖 **10**
page 439
Assignments

Above all, it is imperative on the assignments you provide that you be clear. Make certain that the students understand the assignment for next week, especially the written piece. This is not difficult; the goal is that they would read the material as best as they can and write a few sentences on what they take them to mean. This is a critical intellectual skill for your students to learn, so make sure that you encourage them in this process. Of course, for those students who might find this difficult, assure them of the intent behind this assignment, and emphasize their understanding of the material being the key, not their writing skills. We want to improve their skills, but not at the expense of their encouragement and edification. Nor, however, do we want to sell them short. Strike to find the midpoint between challenge and encouragement here.

Excellence is to be expected from your students, and of course, we know that students will have different abilities to do intellectual work – reading, writing, and so on. While we want to emphasize credible academic performance, we do not wish to exalt these indicators over softness of heart, readiness to obey the Word of God, and availability to serve Christ as he leads by the Spirit. *Constantly monitor your own emphasis on grades, assignments and academic performance. These are important, but not all-important.* Focus on the main thing: unconditional availability to Christ to obey him in our lives as he directs us.

3

URBAN MISSION

LESSON
4

Doing Justice and Loving Mercy
Let Justice Roll Down – The Vision and Theology of the Kingdom

📖 1

page 441
Lesson Introduction

Welcome to the Mentor's Guide for Lesson 4, *Doing Justice and Loving Mercy: Let Justice Roll Down – The Vision and Theology of the Kingdom.* The overall focus of this lesson is to provide you with missional, theological, and strategic foundation to this important ministry in the life of the urban Christian leader. We are exposed to the issues of communities which have been historically subject to a litany of chronic social problems, spiritual oppressions, economic exploitation, and moral compromise. To be an urban Christian leader is synonymous with being a messenger of the justice, mercy, and peace of Jesus Christ, and the church in which he or she serves is the literal outpost and embassy of the Kingdom of God, a rule known by its justice and mercy. In order to benefit from this lesson, you must embrace this vision as your own, that is, you must see that a critical element in your understanding and application of this material is your ability to visualize yourself as a leader for justice and peace, and the church where you worship and serve Christ as a center for that same justice and mercy. Without your own acceptance of this passion in your own life as mentor, you will be severely limited in your ability to help your students embrace this as their own vision.

As you discuss the various concepts, questions, and issues that arise from the material in this lesson, it will be important for you to stay cognizant of how central this theme of demonstrating justice and loving mercy truly is. In many ways this entire lesson is an attempt to understand and to flesh out the simple yet powerful admonition of Micah 6.6-8, an analysis and injunction which summarizes what God would have his person and people to become and to do.

> Mic. 6.6-8 – With what shall I come before the Lord, and bow myself before God on high? Shall I come before him with burnt offerings, with calves a year old? [7] Will the Lord be pleased with thousands of rams, with ten thousands of rivers of oil? Shall I give my firstborn for my transgression, the fruit of my body for the sin of my soul? [8] He has told you, O man, what is good; and what does the Lord require of you but to do justice, and to love kindness, and to walk humbly with your God?

This text is a summary judgment about the kind of service and worship that the Lord desires and demands. On the one hand, God is

URBAN MISSION
4

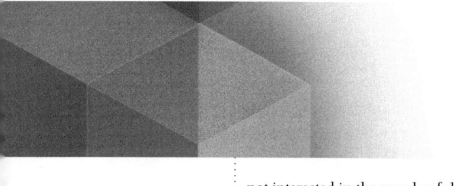

not interested in the wooden fulfillment of ritualistic obedience in an outward, formalistic manner. Rather, God wants the outward expression of an inward passion concerning his will and its fulfillment in our relationship with him and others. God asks that his people act justly, that is, that they express fairness and rightness in all of their dealings with others, that they love mercy, expressing authentic care and compassion in all facets of their relationships with others, and finally, walk humbly with their God, relating to God in gratitude and humility based upon his gracious covenant and care. God desires this throughout the Scriptures, so the demands here are neither novel nor scarce:

> Deut. 10.12-13 – And now, Israel, what does the Lord your God require of you, but to fear the Lord your God, to walk in all his ways, to love him, to serve the Lord your God with all your heart and with all your soul, [13] and to keep the commandments and statutes of the Lord, which I am commanding you today for your good?

> 1 Sam. 15.22 – And Samuel said, "Has the Lord as great delight in burnt offerings and sacrifices, as in obeying the voice of the Lord? Behold, to obey is better than sacrifice, and to listen than the fat of rams."

> Prov. 21.3 – To do righteousness and justice is more acceptable to the Lord than sacrifice.

> Isa. 1.16-19 – Wash yourselves; make yourselves clean; remove the evil of your deeds from before my eyes; cease to do evil, [17] learn to do good; seek justice, correct oppression; bring justice to the fatherless, plead the widow's cause. [18] "Come now, let us reason together," says the Lord: "though your sins are like scarlet, they shall be as white as snow; though they are red like crimson, they shall become like wool. [19] If you are willing and obedient, you shall eat the good of the land."

> Isa. 58.6-11 – Is not this the fast that I choose: to loose the bonds of wickedness, to undo the straps of the yoke, to let the oppressed go free, and to break every yoke? [7] Is it not to share your bread with the hungry and bring the homeless poor into your house; when you see the naked, to cover him, and not to hide yourself from your own flesh?

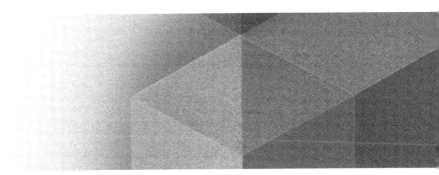

[8] Then shall your light break forth like the dawn, and your healing shall spring up speedily; your righteousness shall go before you; the glory of the Lord shall be your rear guard. [9] Then you shall call, and the Lord will answer; you shall cry, and he will say, "Here I am." If you take away the yoke from your midst, the pointing of the finger, and speaking wickedness, [10] if you pour yourself out for the hungry and satisfy the desire of the afflicted, then shall your light rise in the darkness and your gloom be as the noonday. [11] And the Lord will guide you continually and satisfy your desire in scorched places and make your bones strong; and you shall be like a watered garden, like a spring of water, whose waters do not fail.

To do justice and to love mercy is the surest way we can offer acceptable worship to God, and prove in fact that we are actually walking humbly with him. Unfortunately, the history of God's leaders and his people are often littered with acts of injustice (cf. Mic. 2.1-2; 3.1-3; 6.11), being selfish and disloyal to our neighbors (Mic. 2.8-9; 3.10-11; 6.12), and walking in arrogance and haughtiness before God (2.3). Our aim in this lesson is to ground the students in the theology of these truths, and probe for implications of them for those living in the city.

The aims of this lesson are bold and important, so please pay careful attention to them. They are clearly stated, carefully integrated throughout the material, and designed for you to emphasize them throughout the lesson, especially during the discussions and interaction with the students. The more you can highlight the objectives throughout the class period, the better the chances are that they will understand and grasp the magnitude of these objectives.

📖 2
page 441
Lesson Objectives

The objectives above are designed to shape the entire learning experience of this lesson. Your philosophy must be to integrate all the various ideas, activities, and issues probed in this lesson around them. They represent, in fact, what we hope the students will retain, understand, recite, and embrace as a result of engaging the data in this lesson. They are critical for all you do, and should be referred to often and discussed throughout.

Do not hesitate, therefore, to discuss these objectives briefly before you enter into the class period. Draw the students attention to the objectives, for, in a real sense, this is the heart of your educational aim for the class period in this lesson. Everything discussed and done ought to point back to these objectives. Find ways to highlight these at every turn, to reinforce them and reiterate them as you go.

📖 **3**
page 441
Devotion

This devotion technically focuses upon the second commandment, Lev. 19.18, "You shall not take vengeance or bear a grudge against the sons of your own people, but you shall love your neighbor as yourself: I am the Lord." To live out and to experience a growing, intimate walk with God will demand that we do justice and love mercy, and express it in the lives of those with whom we come into contact. We express this neighbor love, this justice and mercy, in the context of specific, particular, and consistent acts of love and mercy to our brothers and sisters, our neighbors, and even our enemies. The idea of being our brother's keeper lies at the heart of what it means to be authentically God-related. To ignore one's brother (neighbor) is to be caught in the web of jealousy, smallness, and cruelty of Cain, who according to John's commentary on the story murdered his brother Abel because his own deeds were evil and his brother's deeds were righteous, 1 John 3.11-15.

To embrace this vision of human interaction as the heart of all true understanding of God is the way to understand John's recurrent refrain on the need to prove and display one's love for God through a love for others (cf. 1 John 4.7-21; John 13.34-35; 15.12; etc.).

As you discuss the truth of the Genesis story with your students, seek to help them understand the correlation of this ancient tale with the injustice and cruelty that is taking place in so many urban communities today. Our only way out of this fog of viciousness is to rediscover this fundamental characteristic of a truly God-conscious person: to be the keeper of one's neighbor and one's brother. At the heart of all true spiritual discernment, this is the central insight into living our lives as leaders who both act justly and demonstrate God's mercy.

4

URBAN MISSION

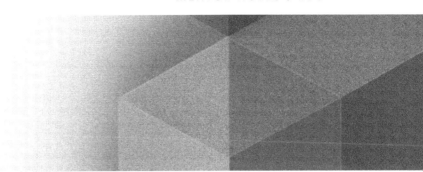

📖 **4**
page 445
Contact

The Contact sections in this lesson were designed to enable your students prepare for the hard intellectual work of considering the vision and theology underlying God's mandate to demonstrate justice and mercy in our lives and through our churches. To investigate the theological data dealing with this, you will need to help your students reflect intentionally on ideas that they normally either take for granted or do not consciously meditate upon very often. Use these questions and ideas to prompt your students to bring to the front of their attention and passions their central questions as they relate to loving others, being loved, and loving God, and how these loves relate to one another, and what the issues and consequences are for failing to demonstrate this justice and mercy to others.

📖 **5**
page 446
Summary

The Concept of the *Imago Dei*

As you explore the meanings of the *imago Dei* with your students, it may be helpful for you to read a nice and concise summary of its major meanings in Scripture from professor Ryken on this critical point:

> Psalm 8 is a classic statement of comparison between God and people. In verse 4 the psalmist's question to God, "What are human beings" (RSV) was generated by his contemplation of the three realities of the inanimate creation, humanness and the divine. The reason the psalmist could even pose this question is that humans are image-bearers of God (Gen. 1.26-27) and are self-aware. Because of the *imago Dei* ("image of God"), the following comparisons can be discerned in Scripture.
>
> At the heart of the imago Dei is personality. God and humans can communicate intelligently together (Ps. 8; Isa. 6.8-13). Both can receive information (Gen. 1.28-30; Heb. 1.1-2), conceive thoughts (Gen. 2.19; 2.23) and process information (Isa. 1.18-20). Although God's knowledge is limitless in accuracy and content (Rom. 11.33-34; Matt. 11.21-24), human knowledge is incomplete (1 Cor. 2.9; 13.12) at its best and twisted at its worst (Eph. 4.17-18). The affective dimension of God (Gen 6.6; Mt 25.21; 2 Cor 7.6) is always perfectly balanced and not dependent

4

URBAN MISSION

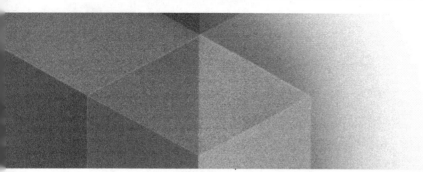

on anyone outside the triune Godhead for its completion (Hos. 11.8-9; Acts 17.25; John 17.24-26). God is the lover who never stops loving (Jer. 31.3; Hos. 11.1-9). Although humans can express noble emotions (Ps. 13.5-6; Mark 12.20-30; 2 Cor. 1.24-2.4; 2 John 4), their love often diminishes (Rev. 2.4), is prostituted by loving the evil (2 Tim. 3.2, 4) and rejoices in the wrong thing (Ps. 13.4; Mic. 3.2; 1 Cor. 13.6). They also give themselves to "degrading passions" (Rom. 1.26). God's choices are always wise and right (Gen. 18.25; Isa. 10.13; Rom. 16.27), whereas human choices are often perverse (Rom. 1.32).

Although there are some overlaps in the following, comparisons are also seen in such areas as character (Isa. 54.5; Hos. 3.1-3; Jer. 5.7, 8; 1 Pet. 1.14, 15), metaphors/similes (John 1.19; Isa. 1.6, 7; Luke 3.22; Matt. 10.16), familial relationships (Jer. 5.7, 8; 31.32; Eph. 5.28; Rev. 21.2) and occupational images (Ps. 23; Zech. 11.17; Matt. 13.55; John 10.11; 1 Cor. 3.5-17; Heb. 11.10; 1 Pet. 5.2). Although time- and space-bound image-bearers (Ps. 90.9-10; 139.7-9) do share some finite continuities with the eternal (Ps. 90.2), unlimited (Ps. 139.7-9), nondependent (Acts 17.25) God, they will always be dependent creatures (Gen. 1.27; Ps. 100.3) in need of other humans (Gen. 2.18), divine information (Matt. 4.4; 1 Cor. 2.6-9) and God himself (John 15.5, 11; 17.3; Ps. 16.5-11; 1 Cor. 6.17).

~ Leland Ryken. *Dictionary of Biblical Imagery.* (electronic ed.). Downers Grove, IL: InterVarsity Press, 2000. pp. 336-337.

📖 6
page 460
Summary of
Key Concepts

The *Summary of Key Concepts* section allows for you to have quick scan of the central ideas, doctrines, and truths covered in the lesson. They represent the fundamental truths of the entire learning sessions written in declarative sentence form. These ideas are meant to be the residual messages of the lesson, that is, those insights which the lesson's study, interaction, and investigation were meant to unearth and make plain to the students. Rehearsing these statements is your way to cement the central ideas of the study sessions in the minds of the students, and provide them with a ready reference to the outline of the lesson. Make sure that these concepts are clearly defined and carefully considered, for their quiz work and exams will be taken from these items directly.

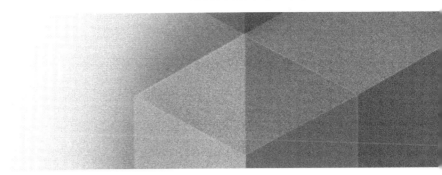

📖 7
page 462
Student Application
and Implications

The *Student Application and Implications* section challenges the student to wrestle with the implications of the lesson for their own life and ministry. It is quite easy for students to forget that the point of our work is not merely to consider ideas, but to connect the content of the lesson to their actual *Sitz im Leben* (German for "situation in life"). Each student must be challenged to ponder the personal ramifications of the truths contained in the lesson for his or her own life, and explore the ideas as they might relate to their own ministry.

Your role, therefore, is to enable your students to think through the central truths with an eye toward their own situations. You may wish to design some questions or use those provided below as water to "prime the pump" of their interests, so to speak. What is significant here is not the questions written below, but for you, in conversation with your students, to settle on a cadre of issues, concerns, questions, and ideas that flow directly from their experience, and relate to their lives and ministries. Do not hesitate to spend the majority of time on some question that arose from the video, or some special concern that is especially relevant in their ministry context right now. The goal of this section is for you to enable them to think critically and theologically in regards to their own lives and ministry contexts. Again, the questions below are provided as guides and primers, and ought not to be seen as absolute necessities. Pick and choose among them, or come up with your own. The key is relevance now, to their context and to their questions.

📖 8
page 468
Assignments

The overall success of the students in a cohort learning situation is for them to learn as they peruse the material individually, as well as when they gather with their fellow students in dialogue, discussion, and prayer. Both individual and group study are significant. Emphasize the need for both individual and group preparation for an insightful and effective learning session.

You will want to make sure that you remind and challenge your students to set aside quality time to fulfill their assignment for next class lesson,

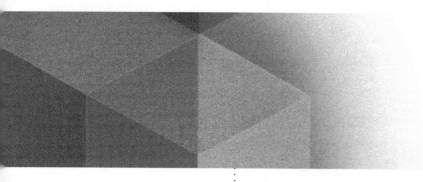

and remind them to pay attention especially to their reading of the material, and the precis (summary) of the written assignment. This is not difficult; the goal is that they would read the material as best as they can and write a few sentences on what they take them to mean. This is a critical intellectual skill for your students to learn, so make sure that you encourage them in this process. Of course, for those students who might find this difficult, assure them of the intent behind this assignment, and emphasize their understanding of the material being the key, not their writing skills. We want to improve their skills, but not at the expense of their encouragement and edification. Nor, however, do we want to sell them short. Strike to find the midpoint between challenge and encouragement here.

Made in the USA
Columbia, SC
23 May 2023